More praise for

THE INNER COAST

and Donovan Hohn

"Donovan Hohn's prose is as immaculate and quotable as that of any writer of his generation. And while you always sense his outrage about ecological calamity, and never doubt his moral engagement, his advocacy never feels hectoring. There's no writer living or dead I would rather read on the reliably distressing topic of environmentalism than Donovan Hohn."

—Tom Bissell

"I've seldom encountered a writer with a better understanding of both the literary and the journalistic ways and means of telling a true story. Donovan Hohn thinks clearly; he writes with eloquence and force."

—Lewis H. Lapham

"Donovan Hohn has a diviner's capacity to tap into the source and the flow of a story, whether the 'story' is narrative or argumentative. His attention to the appearances of things—the false; the true—tunes the reader's alert-addled animal brain to the meaningful, and the terrible. As the Earth begins to resist us, to remind us that how we're living will be our undoing, Hohn's work is that sad, happy thing glinting in the sand: evidence of what a human mind could do, and what a human heart could yield."

—Wyatt Mason

"[Hohn] seems to have it all: deep intelligence, a strikingly original voice, [and] humility."

—Elizabeth Royte, *New York Times Book Review*

THE
INNER
COAST

~

ESSAYS

DONOVAN HOHN

W. W. NORTON & COMPANY
Independent Publishers Since 1923

For information about permission to reproduce selections from this book, write to
Permissions, W. W. Norton & Company, Inc., 500 Fifth Avenue, New York, NY 10110

For information about special discounts for bulk purchases, please contact
W. W. Norton Special Sales at specialsales@wwnorton.com or 800-233-4830

Manufacturing by LSC Communications, Harrisonburg
Book design by Chris Welch Design
Production managers: Lauren Abbate and Erin Reilly

ISBN: 978-1-324-00597-1 (pbk.)

W. W. Norton & Company, Inc., 500 Fifth Avenue, New York, N.Y. 10110
www.wwnorton.com

W. W. Norton & Company Ltd., 15 Carlisle Street, London W1D 3BS

1 2 3 4 5 6 7 8 9 0

For Matthew Power

1974–2014

and Hannah Frank

1984–2017

We look at the world once, in childhood.

The rest is memory.

—"NOSTOS," LOUISE GLÜCK

Contents

Introduction

We are born into stories already in progress—those our families tell or avoid telling; those recorded in history books and newspapers, or left out of them; those encrypted in biomes and geographies, even in our bodies. Every word we read or write carries with it, like vestigial mutations in a strand of DNA or like the isotopes recorded in the ear bone of a fish or like the chemical signatures preserved in a core sample of glacial ice, the history of its usage. We are surrounded by a multitude of facts whose significance is neither stable nor self-evident. "Doubtful certainties," the writer Guy Davenport called such facts.

Twenty years ago, a job as a magazine fact-checker provided me with an apprenticeship in the methods of nonfiction. It taught me to be scrupulous about the details, to distinguish between credible sources and flimsy ones, to be suspicious of superlatives and round numbers, but it also made me sensitive to what I've come to think of as the registers of facts. The register of childhood memories differs from the register of your recollections of this morning's commute. The register of a text message to a confidante differs from the register of an affidavit. Essays, so long as they register the differences, can admit speculations and fantasies and dreams—which are also facts, doubtful certainties as real to us as those we can detect with an MRI scan or stub our toes on.

Over the years, because I'm the writer in my family of origin, I've received from far-flung relations assorted documents and artifacts, become the curator of a haphazard family archive. Not long ago, moving house, I found a box sent to me by an uncle that I hadn't bothered to open when it arrived. I ripped off the packing tape and out tumbled envelopes of photographs, newspaper clippings, letters. My uncle—my mother's youngest brother— had salvaged these findings from among his deceased parents' belongings. The photographs—black-and-white family snapshots, mostly—were loose and jumbled, in no particular order. Many of them had been plucked from the weird scrapbooks my grandfather had kept. A colonel in the Army Air Forces who in civilian life had been a jazz trumpeter, in his scrapbooking my grandfather was more freestyle collage artist than archivist. He'd scissored up photos, glued one atop another, or arrayed around them documents he'd also attacked with his scissors. I found a letter, dated May 21, 1944, sent from an air force base "somewhere in Italy," that my grandfather, between bombing runs, had written to my mother, his firstborn child, on the occasion of her first birthday. He was sorry he couldn't be with her but promised he'd be home soon. Reading the letter, I couldn't help thinking of stories I'd heard from other sources, about my grandfather's temper and the bruises he left on his children. In 1944, thinking of his homecoming, he'd imagined only domestic bliss. "When that day rolls around, just you and mommy and I will be together all by ourselves! And will we ever have fun!" he wrote. "I'll just tickle you so much you won't have a chance to hide those big pearls of yours!"

In another envelope I found a xeroxed copy of the program—printed in both English and Korean—for a concert the Seoul Symphony Orchestra had performed on April 27, 1958. The evening's program had included a trumpet solo played by my grandfather and a piano duet performed by my mother and her sister, who in April of 1958 would have been fourteen and twelve, respectively. I'd heard about this duet many times from relations who'd mentioned it to me as evidence of my mother's hidden gifts and former life. Although the program didn't specify, I knew from my informants which score they'd chosen to play: Gershwin's *Rhapsody in Blue.* With the program were photographs, scissored and still sticky with glue, of the two girls in their matching long skirts and matching ponytails tied back with matching ribbons, seated side by side at the keyboard of the grand piano while their father in his colonel's uniform looks on. When I was growing up, we had a piano in our living room, a Schafer & Sons upright, but except when she was teaching us arpeggios and scales, I don't remember ever hearing my mother play.

I kept shuffling and came upon a letter she'd written to her parents during her first semester at a "women's college" in Milwaukee. My father had recently paid a visit, courting her. She'd met his train, escorted him to his room at the Y. They'd gone for ice cream, caught a showing of *Breakfast at Tiffany's,* whose star, Audrey Hepburn, my mother in her youth slightly resembled. The film, in her opinion, "wasn't too hot." My parents have now been divorced for almost four decades, and my mother, age seventy-six, lives alone in a condo complex in exurban Connecticut where, supported by disability checks, she watches Fox News and types inflamed emails about immigrants.

Most of the newspaper clippings in the box my uncle had

sent—scissored from papers like the *Hastings Daily Tribune* and the *Council Bluffs Nonpareil* (motto: "the key to southwest Iowa")—reported on an epic bike trip my mother had taken at age twenty-one, in 1963, a bike trip I write about in the second-to-last essay collected here. She'd pedaled from Wisconsin to California, from what I've come to think of as the inner coast of the continent to what—in the national mythos, the westering geography of the American imagination—has, since 1849 if not before, been its outermost one, the coast of the Pacific. I was born and raised there, in San Francisco, but spent my childhood traveling between those two coasts—between the City by the Bay and an old family farm near Lake Michigan where my mother's kin gathered for reunions.

By the 1970s, the farm was no longer operational. The family had held on to it as a kind of heritage site to which the increasingly scattered tribe would make pilgrimages, sharing meals of boiled walleye and potato salad while communing nostalgically with an agrarian past, vestiges of which survived. The place was like a museum of anachronisms. Exhibits included: An empty red barn. An outhouse with a splintered door. A hand pump that drew water from a well. Glistening helixes of amber flypaper that spiraled from the farmhouse rafters. There were also a few chickens, including one whose beheading I was made to witness as an initiation into the sort of brutal yet valuable knowledge farm life was thought to impart. Headless, the chicken's body ran a single flapping lap around the chopping block—a feat both gruesome and comical.

At the edge of the farm was a shallow body of water called Lost Lake, and according to legend a logger had, one winter, attempted to drive an oxen team across it. Heavy with harvested timber, his wagon had supposedly broken through thin ice, dragging the logger and oxen with it, a fate I compulsively thought about while paddling around with my brother in a dented aluminum canoe. Lost Lake was so shallow you could touch bottom with your paddle, but the bottom was so silty and soft the paddle blade would sink into it as far as you could plunge it, never touching hard ground. Who knew what was down there. I imagined that if you fell overboard and tried to stand, you'd get sucked into the muck, disappearing like one of those hapless and unlikely prehistoric animals—miniature horses with cloven hooves, saber-toothed tigers—that had mistaken the La Brea Tar Pits for a watering hole and ended up drowned and entombed, which is perhaps how it had gone for that logger and his oxen. An illustrated encyclopedia of the prehistoric mammals of North America was among my prized possessions, and although I'd never visited them, the La Brea Tar Pits were a prominent feature on the landscape of my inner life.

Not long ago my mother and her siblings sold off their share of the ancestral farm. They and their offspring—my generation—were too scattered and estranged to carry on with reunions. I do not miss the place, but on my own, I've kept returning to the Great Lakes. I began working on the first drafts of the earliest essays this book collects as a graduate student in Ann Arbor. A decade later, after publishing a book and becoming a father, I returned to essay-writing and to Michigan, which is where I live now.

~

All coasts are marginal and messy places, which is why people like me are drawn to them, I suspect. Where land and water mingle and meet, so do habitats, biomes, worlds. The heart of the great ocean gyres are biological deserts, but at their edges, where currents collide with coasts, upwelling and down-welling churn up nutrients that fertilize the food chain. In the language of ecology, coasts are biologically productive. Tidal littoral zones teem. So do coastal estuaries. So do the wetlands of riparian floodplains. Underwater, on land, and by air, coasts serve as migration corridors. Animals travel them, and prior to the invention of rail, so did we, which is to say that coasts are culturally as well as biologically productive. Coasts have always been contact zones between *here* and *elsewhere*.

Etymologically, the word "coast" derives from the Latin for "rib," and in Middle English, butchers could still offer you a coast of lamb—meaning a rack of ribs. A seacoast was the rib-cage of the land. In its primary sense, "coast" still refers to the place where land ends and sea begins. In that sense, all coasts are by definition outer and oceanic ones. The usual term for the edge of a lake or stream is "bank" or "shore." But the mari-time geography of the Midwestern interior is a paradox. Mich-igan is Midwestern. It's also coastal—peninsular, in fact. Its shoreline—as speckled with antique lighthouses as New Eng-land's—is longer than California's, Florida's, and that of every other state besides Alaska. Standing on a Midwestern beach, you can watch freighters slide across the horizon. In nauti-cal terms, "to coast" is *to travel by water while keeping the land nearby*, and in that sense, you can coast through the heart of North America, circumnavigating all of the states east of the Mississippi without ever laying eyes on the Pacific.

These days, the word "coastal" is as sociological as it is geo-graphic. In phrases like "coastal living" or "coastal elites," the word collapses the West Coast and East into a conjoined seaboard supposedly inhabited by decadent sophisticates, as if Brooklyn were next door to Berkeley, or Boston in commuting distance of Seattle. Certain Chicagoans or holiday-goers on Michigan's Gold Coast might qualify as coastal in this sense, but not the residents of Gary or Sandusky or Milwaukee; or of Dearborn, home to the largest Muslim community in the United States, which is an afternoon's paddle down the Rouge River from Lake Erie; or of Osborn, a neighborhood on the northeast side of Detroit that has become popular with Hmong immigrants from Vietnam.

In 1615, Samuel de Champlain followed the Ottawa River deep into the interior. From native informants, he'd heard of a "great salt sea" to the west, which he took to be the Pacific. Hoping to reach the continent's outermost coast, he instead made it only as far as the eastern shores of Lake Huron. In his journals he says little about his arrival, on August 1, 1615, at the water's edge. The term he used for the Great Lake, *mer douce*, or sweetwater sea, suggests he may have experienced some confusion. His most recent biographer detects disappointment. Perhaps by the time he arrived, he'd already learned from locals that the Pacific was nowhere nearby, but I like to imagine him on the coast of Lake Huron's Georgian Bay, looking out at the horizon, hoping that China lay on the far side of it, and then kneeling down to take a sip. The water's taste—fresh, not salty—would have been to him at once disillusioning and bewildering, like waking from a dream. I imagine him staggering to his feet, looking around, wondering where he was.

In two of the essays this book collects, I quote the pair of questions that Thoreau asked after ascending Mount Katahdin in Maine, questions that were for him inseparable, the answer to the one depending on the answer to the other: "*Who* are we? *where* are we?" In childhood, when the boundaries between self and world are especially permeable, I think we all ask versions of those questions, but in the first-person singular: "*Who* am I? *where* am I?" Trying to make sense of the stories, histories, and geographies I happened to have been born into, following the compass needle of my curiosity, over the past two decades, I've visited—on foot or in my mind—sites that seemed to me magnetic with mystery or meaning. Thanks to accidents of ancestry and biography, many of those sites have clustered along the two coasts, outermost and innermost, Pacific and Midwestern, between which my imagination has often traveled. With my brushes and sampling jars, by which I mean my notebook and voice recorder, I've collected evidence, arranging doubtful certainties into essays. Thoreau's questions are still good ones, I think. At a time of bewildering and accelerating changes to habitats and geographies, they continue to invite new answers. What follows are several of mine.

—Ann Arbor, Michigan, 2019

THE
INNER
COAST

SNAIL PICKING

I was, at age nine, a god of snails. On the quiet San Francisco cul-de-sac where my family lived, *Helix aspersa*, the brown garden snail, was by far the most plentiful and least evasive wildlife around. Snails plied the long green fins of our neighbor's agapanthus like barges transiting green canals. I'd unglue them from their shiny trails, hold them in midair, and poke their sensitive horns. They'd ripple and recoil.

Usually, I'd show mercy, restoring them to their universe of leaves, but sometimes I'd hurl them hard against a garage door, where they left ichorous spots. Snails were pests, after all. Other times, I'd launch them high above the telephone wires. Diminishing as they rose, they'd hang, suspended for a moment, at the apogee of gravity's arc, little spinning cosmonauts, brown specks on a canvas sky. Watching them, I tried to imagine how it might feel—ganglia lit up like filaments—in that last, astonished instant before they fell. Did they experience snail terror? Snail rapture? Or were they too dumb and dizzy to experience anything at all? Afterward, on the asphalt, the shattered bubbles of their bodies, veiny and blue, reminded me of the skinned testicle I'd glimpsed while browsing my father's medical books.

One day I filled a half-gallon margarine tub with snails,

took them home, and set them on my nightstand. Glowing jars of fireflies were for other children. For me, a tub of snails. They climbed the white, translucent walls and clung to the underside of the perforated lid. From my pillow, before turning out my light, I could see their dark forms moving around like thoughts. When I awoke the next morning, the lid was off, and the tub, save for a dozen gray squiggles of turd, was empty. Only after opening the curtains did I spy the slow explosion happening all over my bedroom walls, the small armada, the wakes of light.

A ROMANCE OF RUST

Inches above the auctioneer, under the humid eaves of an almost empty shed, wasps bounce as if on strings, tending their paper nests. "Folks, I've been doing this for thirty-five years," the auctioneer barks into his wireless headset. His voice, amplified by two portable speakers, crackles across the afternoon. "First thing I ever auctioned was a birdcage. It sold for a dollar twenty-five. Bidding went up by a quarter back then." He is a short man with a big gut and a scrunched face, the face of a circus clown without his makeup on. His denim newsboy cap matches his denim suspenders. "God's been good to us so far," he observes, interrupting his banter to gaze anxiously at the horizon to the west. "But I'd better hurry. I want to beat the rain."

After one of the longest winters in recent memory, spring has finally arrived in Lower Michigan, a fitful, moody spring full of sudden changes. Last night a thunderstorm scattered hailstones across Washtenaw County. Now the sun is out, steam is rising off the fields of timothy and winter wheat, and the air smells pleasantly of mud. If it does start raining again, Tom Friedlander will likely hold the auctioneer personally responsible. All day Tom has been complaining about this clown's lack of professionalism, his fondness for banter, his ignorance of tools. "He has no idea what he's selling," Tom keeps whispering to me. A real professional, he says, would be done by now.

Atop one of three hay wagons, a skinny teenage boy with a crew cut stoops to the rusty junk piled at his feet and hoists a bow saw into the air. It is an exquisite specimen, just like the ones I've seen in books. "Lift her up nice and high, Ben," the auctioneer says. Bow saws are shaped like the harps angels play in comic strips. They are both ingenious and primitive, held together by the tension in a twisted loop of rope.

"Howaboutabid, twenty," the auctioneer chants. "I've got twenty. Howaboutabid, twenty-five-five-five? Twenty-five. Twenty-seven-and-a-half? Now thirty. Thirty, thirty, thirty?"

People have been using versions of the bow saw for hundreds of years, but not until the turn of the twentieth century, when motorized jigsaws were rendering them obsolete, did anyone think to salvage them from the scrap heap and preserve them for posterity. For decades, this particular saw was as valuable as it was useful to the farmer who owned it. Then one day the farmer grows too old to farm, his children excavate the moldering contents of his barn, hire an auctioneer, the auctioneer runs advertisements in local papers and in *Auction Exchange,* drags the saw out into the sunlight along with the rest of the farmer's belongings—rakes with broken handles, a wall clock made out of a slab of polished wood, nails fused by rust into pointy lumps—and the next thing you know, you could have purchased ten new saws for what this useless one is selling for.

Earlier that morning, while we were inspecting the contents of the hay wagons, an old lady wiggled what looked to be a miniature iron hoe at Tom and asked him what it was.

"That's an ash rake," he informed her. "For emptying ashes from a stove."

"I don't have a stove," the old lady replied, sensibly, "so I don't need it."

Like her, most people imagine that the form of a tool is a pure expression of its function and that its value is a measure of its usefulness. Saws cut. Hammers pound. On the antique-tool market, however, value is largely aesthetic and symbolic. Hammers do not only pound, saws do not only cut. They also *mean*.

As the bow saw transubstantiates from a piece of junk into a collectible before our eyes, Tom Friedlander listens closely to the ascendant bids, stroking his beard, but stays out of it. Bow saws aren't his thing. Too pricey. Too desirable. Ever since bidding began several hours ago, he has kept his head down, except when he wants to catch the auctioneer's eye. To place a bid, he will glance up, nod gravely, and curl his fingers toward his heart, beckoning. So far today he has purchased a hand-forged chopper, a barn-beam auger, two antique motor-oil bottles with cone-shaped spouts, a box of early automobile starter cranks, a set of speed wrenches, a fence stretcher, something called the Tox-O-Wik cattle oiler, and a plastic bucket full of implement wrenches marinating in melted hail.

"I've got fifty," calls the auctioneer, "fifty-five-five-five, fifty-seven-and-a-half."

If a few years ago you had asked me what I thought of tool-collecting, I would have told you that it sounded like the sort of sentimental pastime pursued mainly by men with soft minds, thick wallets, and lonely wives. In New York, where I lived at the time, one sometimes encountered woodworking tools and farming implements on the walls of pastorally themed restaurants serving expensive comfort food, or among handmade quilts and kerosene lanterns in the windows of West Village boutiques. I considered such Americana to be so much nostalgic gimcrack. The inflated prices old tools commanded I attributed to an ambient dissatisfaction with modernity. The more expendable we felt in our jobs, the more complicated and computerized our lives became, the more hardware made of metal and wood seemed to symbolize all that we had lost—we Americans, but especially we American men.

Until recently in America, manliness was proportionate to handiness. The ancient Greeks had Achilles and his shield. The British had Arthur and Excalibur. We had John Henry and his hammer, Paul Bunyan and his axe, Queequeg and his manly harpoon. Our national poets sang hymns to the broad axe and the village blacksmith. Our prophets didn't merely wander in the wilderness; they built cabins there. The adzes and bow saws with which anxiety-beset urban professionals now equip their apartments originally belonged to self-reliant, self-employed, self-made yeomen and artisans—or so the traffickers in nostalgia wished us to believe.

It was a lie, I knew, this Luddite fantasy of an artisanal golden age. That legendary Yankee ingenuity was born not only out of an ardor for craftsmanship and independence but also out of a shortage of skilled labor and an abundance of cheap, pilfered land. European settlers had picked up many of their tricks (hollowing a canoe with fire, fertilizing corn with fish) from natives whom they repaid with alcohol and infectious disease.

And besides, mowing a field of hay by hand was backbreaking work, nothing romantic about it. Homespun textiles required endless, mind-numbing cottage industry. Likewise the churning of butter, the curing of meat, the hewing of beams and chiseling of mortises. No wonder so many of our agrarian forebears fled to cities at the first chance they got, or else bet the farm on motorized combines and harvesters.

I also had personal reasons to be suspicious of tool-collecting. Although I come from a family of insufferably handy men— men able to wire a house, rebuild a transmission, or frame a wall without calling an expert or consulting a book—I am profoundly unhandy. By the traditional measures of American manhood, I am, essentially, a Frenchwoman. When my brother and I were teenagers, he and our father would adjourn to the garage after dinner, hook a cage light to the underside of an elevated hood, and spend hours passing tools back and forth, while upstairs I lay on the couch reading mildly pornographic fantasy novels. To this day, when I do it myself, I can never be sure whether I am improving my home or conducting experiments upon it.

One might, therefore, find it strange or worrisome that for a year and a half I've devoted every waking hour I could spare to the study of old tools. I've read books with titles like *Wrenches: Antique and Unusual* and *The Hammer: The King of Tools*. I've stayed up all night browsing the searchable archives of the U.S. Patent and Trademark Office, encountering there such exotic utensils as the Clamp Fur-Knife, which, when "Edward Flint, of the city, county, and State of New York," invented it in 1837, was "a new and useful Instrument for Extracting Hairs from Fur-Skins," and I have met a vice president of innovation and design in the cafeteria of the Stanley Works corporate headquarters in New Britain, Connecticut. I've lurked in chat rooms with discussion threads devoted to such subjects as "A previously unknown Albert Goodell brace found in the wild." One sweltering summer morning, on the Jay County fairgrounds in the farming village of Portland, Indiana, I walked among fabulous machines as small as schnauzers and as huge as elephants, all gleaming in the August sun. Drive belts whirred, flywheels revolved, pistons fired, and a forest of smokestacks piped foul smoke and rude music into the otherwise cloudless sky. Mostly, I have ridden a Midwestern circuit of flea markets and farm auctions in the passenger seat of an emerald-green Toyota pickup truck piloted by a fifty-five-year-old botanist with a ponytail, spectacles like windowpanes, and a beard verging on the Whitmanesque.

Tom Friedlander is a tall, faintly melancholy man, prone to long silences and outbursts of goofiness, whom I have always known as Uncle Tom. In 1976, after the botany department of the University of Michigan declined to approve his doctoral dissertation, a taxonomical study of the gray dogwood, for which he had spent the better part of three years scouring the continent for specimens, Tom joined his wife, Martha, my father's sister, on the faculty of a high school in Ann Arbor. The two have taught biology there ever since. Childless and frugal, by the late 1980s they had saved enough to purchase a ranch house in the rural exurbs, along with the thirty-seven acres of marshy, unprofitable farmland adjoining it, which they subsequently let run wild. For years, Martha had been inviting me to visit this nature sanctuary of theirs.

Upon first entering the house, I'd stopped short. Strung on wires and depending from nails hung thousands, or maybe even tens of thousands, of keys. Some strands drooped in elliptical wreaths. Others contorted themselves into asymmetrical Möbius strips and figure eights. The longest strands described arcs across the wallpaper like bunting. The shortest bristled in shiny bouquets. Later, I asked Tom about these peculiar wall hangings. At auctions and flea markets, he explained, dealers sold old tools by the box, and when he returned from his weekend tool hunts, he often found keys buried at the bottom, "like prizes." So he saved them. "People just give them away." Holding a length of keys out for my inspection, he thumbed its tarnished contents. Didn't I see how different they all were? Their lengths and shapes? The words and numbers stamped onto their variegated surfaces?

Tom led me down half a flight of stairs to the television den, where a mob of brass hose nozzles had stormed the mantelpiece and platoons of stove-plate handles flanked the wood-burning stove. Other objects had been mounted according to kind on graying scraps of plywood, which leaned about the room— against bookshelves, in corners—like canvases about a painter's studio. There was a board containing sillcocks, those spigot handles shaped like cross sections of bell pepper, some of them red, some blue, some green, some rusty and bare. Other boards contained screwdrivers, locks, showerheads. A few contained rusty things I failed to recognize. A bandolier of belt buckles dangled from a hook originally intended for a houseplant. On an end table beside a row of matching conch shells lay a pair of eggs—fluted, geometric oblongs of speckled glass. Electrical insulators, Tom explained, from telephone lines.

He referred to these taxonomical arrays of his as "experiments." When he retired from teaching, he would make more of them, he said, many, many more of them, so he could hang them on walls where visitors could see them and "old-timers" could come and talk to him about his tools, maybe even identify some of the "whatsits," those objects whose original purpose had become mysterious.

As is true of many people who spend their days working with kids, there is something perennially youthful about Tom. At family reunions when I was a child, he would tell my brother and me that he kept things in his beard—coins, bluebird eggs—and then he'd bend down so that, half-believing him, we could investigate its scratchy depths. He'd catch insects with his bare hands and tell us their names, both Latin and common, as well as their secrets—why fireflies lit up or why cicadas left their exoskeletons on the trunks of my grandmother's trees. He'd seemed omniscient to me then, wizard-like. He could recite entire Monty Python routines by heart, as well as long portions of *The Hitchhiker's Guide to the Galaxy*, and he sometimes spoke in peculiar voices, impersonating robots or masters of kung fu. He said things like, "Take this marble from my hand, Grasshopper, and your training will be complete."

That afternoon in his television den, I asked Tom how large his tool collection was, and he led me to his study, which contained a library of botanical texts with titles like *Trees, Shrubs, and Woody Vines of the Southwest*, or *Botanical Microtechnique*, or *World Without Trees*. On the other side of the room, homemade bookshelves teetered under the weight of old hardware catalogues and reference books about tools, such as P. T. Rathbone's *History of Old Time Farm Implement Companies and the Wrenches They Issued* and Eric Sloane's classic *A Museum of Early American Tools*. From a nail in the doorway hung a clipboard, to which was clipped a stack of sheets. This was Tom's inventory. Whenever he returned from a tool hunt, he added his new quarry to the running tally. He'd acquired his first old tool by mistake while shopping for a hole punch at the local Kiwanis thrift store. The box lot that contained the punch he wanted also happened to contain a foot-long engineer's wrench. A few months later, discovering an identical wrench at an antiques store, he experienced what he describes as "an instant vision of symmetry." That was 1988. By March 2002, when I first visited his home, he had accumulated, and rudimentarily classified, approximately 25,000 formerly useful things, not counting the keys. Almost 18,000 were wrenches (Tom's specialty), a few thousand were screwdrivers, and several hundred were soldering irons. The exhibit in the television den represented only a small sample. "The rest," Tom told me, "are in the barn."

Southeast Michigan can be beautiful in leaf or under snow, but that winter it had hardly snowed at all, and the Friedlanders' nature sanctuary was a desiccated, khaki-colored wasteland. The silver blimp of a propane tank glowed between the bare branches of bushes planted to obscure it. Behind the house, where corn once grew, an ocean of goldenrod—still brown and dormant—stretched to the woodlot on the horizon. On the way to the tool barn, we passed the greenhouse Tom and Martha had built out of corrugated fiberglass. Two plastic barrels full of frozen rain stood sentry beside the entrance. Inside, I could discern the shadowy forms of succulents (one of Tom's previous taxonomical obsessions) weathering the hostile biome in balmy serenity.

Although there was a barn-sized barn on the property—

a dilapidated cavern full of owl shit, darkness, and mildewy hay where Tom kept the antique tractor he used to mow paths through the goldenrod in the summer and plow the driveway in the winter—the prefabricated steel structure in which he stored his tools was scarcely bigger than a two-car garage. We entered through a side door, stepping awkwardly over three metal spheres huge as medicine balls while fluorescent tubes flickered on overhead.

My first impression was an abstraction: I did not see the hundreds of handsaws hanging from pegs like keys in a locksmith's shop, or the iron shoe lasts arranged in pigeonholes according to size, or the towering steel file cabinets with handwritten tags taped above their handles, or the railroad jacks congregating on a shelf, or the flock of meat scales and wooden pulleys suspended from the ceiling by hooks; what I saw was the idea of multitude. *Be fruitful and multiply,* the Lord had commanded, and we had, we Americans; here all around us was our labor's rusty fruit.

"There are over five hundred drawers full of stuff in here," Tom told me. "That's the sort of scale. Plus the walls. Plus the floor. Plus containers. It's all organized. For instance, this is the overflow hammer drawer." He yanked open the drawer in question. Wooden hafts lay atop one another like matches in a matchbox. Tom selected a mallet with a head like a half-melted marshmallow and held it up for my inspection. The beaten surface of its polls was fissured with tiny cracks like the hide of an elephant. "Lead hammer," Tom said. He returned it with a clatter to the drawer and selected another. "Composition hammer." And another. "Farrier's horseshoe nail-driving hammer."

Here and there, weighted down beneath whatever tool was

most proximate, were pages torn from spiral notebooks on which Tom had catalogued the contents of his five hundred drawers, all of which he seemed to have memorized. If an item caught my eye and I asked him about it, he could almost always identify it by name and purpose, and when he couldn't, his eyes shone with excitement. "That," he would pronounce, "is a whatsit." The steel balls we'd climbed over upon entering were whatsits, though Tom did have a theory about them: They might be ball bearings from the gun turret of a battleship.

As we made our way slowly down the crowded aisles, what struck me most was how zoological Tom's tools seemed, especially the more exotic ones. Divorced from usefulness and subjected to morphological classification, they looked like the fossils of Cenozoic mollusks or the wristbones of tyrannosaurs. Certain pliers bore striking resemblances to the beaks of birds, certain wrenches to the jaws of lizards. The points of chisels and awls looked like talons and claws. Even the names of tools suggested zoological comparisons; there was a goosewing axe, an alligator wrench, a mortising twivil called a *bec d'âne,* French for "nose of a donkey." Loggers had once assembled their rafts with oversized staples known as "dogs." It is, in fact, impossible to talk about tools without resorting to biological metaphors. We refer to the "head" and "claw" of a hammer, the "frog" and "throat" of a plane, the "jaws" of a vise, the "eye" of an adze.

This had to be what motivated Tom's manic collecting. He wasn't merely a collector of tools; he was a taxonomist of tools, a *naturalist* of tools. He'd progressed from gray dogwoods to succulents to wrenches, as if the age-old distinction between nature and culture were the folly of philosophers. I could feel my mind begin to fizz with grandiose, half-baked notions.

Everything evolves, I thought. *Even hammers. Even keys.* I mentioned the zoological analogy, and Tom began rummaging through drawers until he found what he was looking for, an adjustable wrench with a distinctly avian silhouette. "The Puffin!" he exclaimed.

Nothing in the barn illustrated this theory of technological Darwinism more dramatically than Tom's wrenches. He'd organized them first by method of manufacture, separating the hand-forged from the drop-forged, then by type, separating crescent from box, socket from implement, ratchet from alligator, monkey from dog bone. Each of these species he'd subdivided further according to the number of their openings, or the material from which they were made, or the specialized purpose they'd served. Some of his specimens represented transitional designs in the evolution of the wrench. Some were technological chimeras that hybridized wrenches with other implements.

Why wrenches? Why tools?

Tom fell quiet, stroking his beard. "I don't know," he said finally. "I guess I just find them beautiful." Although he could extemporize animatedly about the history of the valve seat grinder, or the art of rope-making, or how long it took to manually drill blast holes into a deposit of coal, aesthetics were another matter. The unlikely beauty of his rusty treasures defied elaboration. His critical vocabulary consisted mainly of the words "neat," "cool," and "fun." Tools he disliked were simply "junk," a term he usually reserved for the cheaply mass-produced, or for a specimen damaged beyond rescue.

His favorite tools dated from the turn of the century, before the consolidation of the hardware industry, when thousands of new mechanical species appeared every year. "Eighteen eighty to 1920, roughly the same time that Michigan was logged over, that was the heyday of tractors," Tom informed me. Because nut and bolt sizes had yet to be thoroughly standardized, every new piece of farm machinery came with its own wrenches, creating the technological equivalent of biodiversity. "After the twenties, mass-produced steel tools came in, and virtually no specialty plow or tractor wrenches were made after that. It all just vanished." As extinctions went, this one seemed hardly worth getting upset over. Who cared about the lost golden age of implement wrenches?

Many collectors and dealers restore their tools, scraping away the rust, polishing the finish. Some will even apply a coat of paint, white for the embossed patent information and brand names, black for the rest. Such adulterations dismay Tom, who prefers used tools to the expensive ones described in auction catalogues as "mint" or "like new." He will clean his finds, but delicately, forensically almost, careful to preserve any "use marks"—the particularizing details that might disclose a tool's secret life. He spoke of his specimens as if they were alive, or had been once. "I loved finding this," he said of a particularly rusty implement wrench. "No serious fine-tool collector would want this, but I want it. Got it for a dollar. What a beautiful wrench. It was under water—a wet place—and it died." The wrench *was* beautiful, though I couldn't have told you why, any more than he could.

I thought of *Let Us Now Praise Famous Men,* the literary documentary in which writer James Agee and photographer Walker Evans illuminate the material lives of tenant farmers in Alabama during the Great Depression. Examining Tom's tools, some of which bore the signatures of blacksmiths, others the stamped initials of extinct railroad companies, still others the tarnished trace of some dead laborer's sweaty palm, I was reminded of the passage in which Agee describes a pair of overalls. "They have begun with the massive yet delicate beauty of most things which are turned out most cheaply in great tribes by machines," Agee writes, "and on this basis of structure they are changed into images and marvels of nature." And yet Agee's had been a scavenger hunt for the present, not for the past. He and Walker Evans had sought "to perceive simply the cruel radiance of what is"—not the quaint glimmer of what was. Where lies the boundary between meaning and sentiment? I wondered. Between memory and nostalgia? America and Americana? What is and what was? Does it move?

Martha appeared in the doorway of the tool barn, summoning us to dinner. Tom turned off the fluorescent lights and padlocked the door. Night had fallen. A city boy since birth, I was used to light-polluted skies. Here, only an hour southwest of Detroit, the stars were as bright and plentiful as in a planetarium show. The Friedlanders' ranch house, lamplight streaming from its windows, looked like a ship adrift upon black swells.

I stayed over that night, and on my way to bed, I stopped in the carpeted hallway where an entire wall had been papered in cartography. From a pushpin in the corner of a particularly enormous map dangled a shoestring. This was, I saw upon inspection, the radius of a vast, Midwestern galaxy the nucleus of which was the Friedlanders' farm. Red hash marks divided the string into increments, counting off miles. Towns throughout Michigan, Indiana, Illinois, Ohio, and Ontario had been circled in felt pen, and dates and distances scrawled beside them. Newspaper advertisements for estate auctions fluttered under pins. "Retired from farming," they typically began, "I will sell the following list..." If the owner of an estate had died, as was often the case, the auctioneers resorted to participles: "Selling personal property of the late Hazel Skriba at public auction..." I unpinned one. The personal property it inventoried—walnut dressers and whippletrees, old magazines and hay forks and Depression glass—read like a kind of material obituary, a portrait of a life in things.

"I've got fifty," calls the auctioneer. "Fifty-five-five-five, fifty-seven-and-a-half."

Ben, the teenage sideman, revolves atop the hay wagon, parading the bow saw like a trophy high above the tipped bills of a hundred baseball caps emblazoned with logos and slogans: RIFKIN SCRAP IRON & METAL CO., I'D RATHER BE HUNTING, WESTPHALIA AUTO SALVAGE, PURINA, GOD BLESS AMERICA, MR. ASPHALT. Across Tom Friedlander's blue ball cap a galleon embroidered from gold thread sails above the legend H.M.S. *Victory.* Most of the auction-goers are elderly farmers; with his ponytail and great Victorian beard, Tom seems as out of place among them as Darwin among the Patagonians. Save for his blue cap, his brown hiking sneakers, and the turquoise decorations on his leather belt, he is dressed entirely in green—green work pants, green work shirt—and vaguely resembles an anthropomorphized plant.

The bow saw finally sells for $87.50, and Ben the teenage sideman next lifts an ink-jet printer into the air. "Something for your computer," the auctioneer says doubtfully. He starts the bidding at fifty dollars but, getting no takers, lowers it: forty dollars, thirty-five dollars, twenty-five, fifteen, ten, seven-and-a-half. Finally, he gives up and banishes it to "the dog pond," a corner of the shed reserved for items no one wants. Only a few years old and still in its original box, the ink-jet printer has already passed into that limbo of worthlessness that exists between novelty and nostalgia.

"Nowadays things are almost obsolete before they leave the drawing board," Eric Sloane, the seminal romancer of antique tools, observed forty years ago. "How lucky we are that so many of the old tools and the things that were made with them were dated and touched with the craftsman's art." Sloane believed that the value of a thing should be a measure of its quality, much as reputation was once regarded as the measure of one's soul. My generation, more narcissistic but also more jaded than his, seems to treasure most the consumerist dross we remember from childhood, irrespective of its inherent worth. In our collecting we are autobiographers, not connoisseurs. I find myself wondering how long it will take before this ink-jet printer escapes the dog pond and ascends to the ranks of the collectible. When he published A Museum of Early American Tools in 1964, Sloane almost single-handedly transformed old tools into Americana. There had been collectors before him, but they were mostly antiquarians and archaeologists who regarded tools as artifacts or aesthetic objects, not sacred relics. At first glance, Sloane's book appears to be nothing more than a pictorial dictionary or field guide. In truth, it is a political tract, an illustrated manifesto of romantic, Yankee conservatism.

The "ancient implements" it depicts, Sloane's dedication

informs us, are not only tools but "symbols of a sincerity, an integrity, and an excellency that the unionized craftsman of today might do well to emulate." His story of decline has no room for tenant farmers, migrant workers, sweatshops, displaced natives, slaves, nor for early Americans who did shoddy work.* The harmony that the "fine craftsman" once felt with his material and tools is, as Sloane describes it, not unlike that which once existed between Adam and the beasts. "An extraordinary awareness of life and time permeated our early days," he writes. Again and again in the commentary that accompanies his old-timey pen-and-ink drawings of apple barrows and hay forks, he praises the craftsmen of yore at the expense of "modern workers," whose "constant aim is more to make the most money from their profession instead of producing the most honest and beautiful and lasting things."

To this day on the antique-tool market, Eric Sloane's romantic biases pertain. Wood sells better than metal, metal better than plastic. Carpentry tools sell better than those of other

---

* In fact, the early Americans Sloane glorifies were on average versatile but mediocre craftsmen compared with the members of European guilds. "Although the rural and small-town economy of the eighteenth century supported a number of specialized artisans," explains Paul B. Kebabian, author of *American Woodworking Tools*, "the majority of the population farmed. And each farmer had to be something of a jack-of-all-trades: he was wagon-maker; house- and barn-builder; maker of hats, cloth, tools, furniture, nails and handspikes, staves and heading and hoops for barrels, potash, maple sugar, or any of a host of other products for use at home and for trade and sale." The abundance and variety of American tools, in fact, testifies to a shortage, not a preponderance, of skill. The carpenter on the *Pequod*, whom Melville describes as "omnitooled," is "to a certain off-handed, practical extent, alike experienced in numerous trades and callings collateral to his own." In addition to maintaining the seaworthiness of the ship, he performs dental surgery, repairs Ahab's prosthetic leg, and decorates the second mate's favorite oar with a constellation of stars.

crafts and trades. The plane, certain rare specimens of which have been known to fetch $20,000 or more, is probably the most collectible tool there is. The wrench, Tom Friedlander's specialty, is among the least.

Devised by carpenters of the Roman Empire, the plane could hypothetically have been used by Jesus Christ himself, before he gave up woodworking for fishing. A hundred years ago a carpenter's tool chest typically would have contained dozens of varieties of planes, and a typical hardware catalogue would list hundreds of varieties (astragals, fillisters, snipe bills, ogees, Grecian ovolos), each one adapted to a highly specialized purpose. Shipwrights smoothed the decks of ships with planes resembling horseshoe crabs, and violinmakers carved fiddle heads with planes, made from lignum vitae, that were smaller than a thumb. Then, at the end of the nineteenth century, what the jigsaw did to the bow saw planing machines did to planes. According to Eric Sloane, in New England in the mid-1900s obsolete planes were being sold as firewood for as little as five dollars a barrel, including the barrel. Only when planes became less plentiful and more mysterious did collectors take interest, suggesting that death may be the mother of nostalgia as well as of beauty. The twilight of the plane was the heyday of the wrench. Leonardo da Vinci is said to have doodled designs for an adjustable wrench in his notebooks; but it was with the invention of bolt-threading machines in the early 1800s that the wrench became as useful and as common as the hammer. In 1869 a writer for *Scientific American,* marveling at how "rude and uncouth" old tools were compared with the machine-lathed wonders of his day, described antebellum wrenches as being mostly of "the pot hook variety." The history of the wrench is the history of industrialism writ small. No matter how many farmers use them, no matter how mechanized agriculture becomes, on the antique-tool market wrenches symbolize pastoralism's antithesis. Of metal for metal, they are the emblem of mechanics and machinists, the standard raised in the fists of factory workers in revolutionary murals. They are the tool of the unionized masses, not the self-reliant yeoman or artisan. Wrenches assemble and adjust; they do not make. There are no wrenches in Eric Sloane's *Museum*.

Time, it seems, is an ironist. That spring, the spring of 2003, factory workers were being laid off in record numbers—Michigan alone had lost 171,000 manufacturing jobs in the previous four years—and the riveters and machine operators Sloane derided seemed like skilled artisans compared with the technicians and sales associates replacing them. The era of the wrench, like the era of the plane before it, is ending. Predictably, the ranks of wrench collectors recently have begun to swell. Although still worth far less than a desirable plane, a rare and pristine John Deere tractor wrench can now fetch hundreds of dollars at auction. Partly this reflects the enthusiasm in rural America for the antique tractors with which such wrenches were originally sold. But the popularity of other wrench varieties—pipe wrenches, automobile wrenches, buggy wrenches, battery cable-pulling wrenches—is also growing. The decline of American manufacturing has given rise to pastoralism's postindustrial analogue: a romance of rust.

I leave Tom beside the hay wagon, a heap of treasures accumulating in the grass at his feet, and survey the premises. Parked in the rutted drive that runs between the house and the barn,

a white camping trailer radiates patriotism and the smell of
boiling kielbasa. NAN'S SNACK WAGON, a sign reads. Plastic
American flags suction-cupped to the trailer's roof scroll and
unscroll themselves listlessly in the humid air. Across the trailer's side, someone has airbrushed this poem:

> Let the Eagle Fly
> Land of the Free
> Home of the Brave
> Love Your Country
> Thank God
> And the Veterans

Through a small concession window at the rear of the trailer
a woman, presumably Nan herself, hands a hot dog to an old
man whose suspenders spell ALASKA in vertical letters. Pro-
truding from the purse of another customer is a leather-bound,
gilt-edged volume titled *Armageddon*.

I hear people speculating about what will happen to this
farm now that the owners have grown too old for it. I hear
rumors of rest homes and funeral parlors, and notice among
the larger items up for auction a motorized wheelchair, an electric hospital bed, a walker, a chamber pot. An estate auction, I
realize, is part festival, part funeral. It's not just the owners of
this farm who are dying but the farm itself. Splotches of lichen
the color of toothpaste bloom everywhere, on the stone foundation of the barn, on the rusty farm equipment—cultipackers,
harrows, plows—spread out like modernist sculpture across
the sodden lawn.

Even in the too-insistent imperatives of the snack wagon's

patriotic hymn, I think I can discern an undertone of foreboding and grief. It's there, too, along with happy chatter about last night's hailstorm, in the conversations of the auction-goers. They walk among old furniture and collectibles as if through lost time. They spin the dial of the Lone Ranger radio and say to their spouses, *look at this, check this out, remember these.* They fondle the porcelain doll with the cracked skull and the jaundiced nightgown, then punch the keys of the old Remington cash register, smiling when the different prices—all charmingly low—spring up behind the little pane of glass.

That summer Tom and I drive to auctions all over Michigan, leaving sometimes as early as sunrise, when fog still eddies between the hills and the shadow of Tom's emerald pickup ripples on the grassy margin beside us. When we return at the end of the day, buckets and boxes of junk bungeed down in the bed of the truck, the shadows are just as long but stretch in the other direction. During fourteen years of collecting, Tom has memorized the state highways. He has his own personal landmarks—a yellow house that glows "like a beacon" from atop a ridge, a pair of boulders that he says are glacial eccentrics, an ice-cream stand called King Kone in the shape of an enormous soft-serve whose new owners no longer offer Tom's favorite flavor, orange-vanilla swirl. Everywhere we go, I see used cars for sale, parked in front lawns atop rectangles of uncropped grass.

Tom likes to get to auctions at least an hour or two early so that he can appraise the day's offerings and search for the treasures that unscrupulous bidders sometimes bury under scrap. This is his favorite part, and watching him rummage through the contents of a table or hay wagon, I think I know why. Here he is most like a naturalist in the field or an archaeologist on a dig. When he finds something that interests him, he holds it to his eyes, inspects it, rubs its finish, tests its moving parts. It wouldn't surprise me if he started tasting things. As he rummages, he provides a running commentary for my benefit: "This is a seed-corn planter. Everybody had one. The American Standard. You put your seed corn in there. You jab it in the ground, and this spring pops open the door as it sinks in and releases one seed at a time."

Other collectors and some auctioneers greet Tom with nods. Regulars on the local auction circuit seem to regard him as a harmless eccentric, a wild man cum nutty-professor figure. Acquaintances and strangers alike bring tools for him to identify. Just as often, though, Tom is the one asking questions. This is how he has learned so much. The intensity with which he listens elicits uncharacteristically voluble explanations from farmers accustomed to silence. His inquisitiveness dignifies the obsolete knowledge they possess, and they proffer it gladly. At the same time, I am surprised by how many of Tom's questions leave his interlocutors dumbfounded. Even recognizable tools baffle: *Sure, it's a hammer, but what was it used for? To break peanut brittle? To tenderize meat? To adjust the inner workings of a watch? See how it's got a little cutter on it?*

Just past sunrise on a June morning, we drive north on M-52, a highway that runs vertically up the mitten of Michigan, farming towns strung along its length like beads. Somewhere between Saginaw and Hemlock, the arrow on a hand-lettered PARKING sign directs us into a pasture where a small contingent of other trucks—up to their wheel hubs in winter wheat, fins of dried mud sprayed across their doors—have already convened. The recently deceased owner of this pasture, a farmer named Dale Krause, was himself an obsessive collector of agro-industrial relics. The list of items up for sale today is varied and long. Bidding will begin at 9 A.M., an hour or two earlier than usual, and may go on past dark. "This is a all day large auction," reads the ad in *Auction Exchange*. "Many of the outbuildings are full with oldies too numerous to mention! Bring your trailers. Be there!!!"

Along with the usual rust-laden hay wagons, the numerous oldies arrayed across the trampled clover this morning include the remains of an old hand loom, a buggy with a bearskin blanket disintegrating on the upholstered seat, and a dozen antique tractors, some of which are as shiny and colorful as brand-new toys and some of which look like partially dissected mechanical cadavers. Amid them towers an elephantine monstrosity of galvanized sheet metal, like something out of Jules Verne or the notebooks of Leonardo da Vinci. This, I learn upon investigation, is a McCormick Deering 38 grain thrasher. Its wheels are made of bare iron. Its drive belt is part metal, part wood. Its bolt heads are not hexagonal but square. Across one side someone has performed mysterious calculations in chalk. "That," Tom says, "should be in the Smithsonian."

By the time the auction begins, three hundred or more vehicles have arrived, nearly all of them pickup trucks. The crowd is so large, two spotters stand in its midst. When they spy a bidder, they shout "Hep!" and point. The auctioneers— there are two of them as well—wear matching white cowboy hats and travel from item to item in a four-wheel John Deere all-terrain vehicle outfitted with loudspeakers and a pulpit, above which, like the drooping head of a dying flower, a yellow, pyramid-shaped parasol dangles from a hook. In Tom's opinion, these guys are "real pros." They know what they're selling and sell it well, which is to say, speedily and honestly.

A farm auction has a discernible shape, a heliotropic arc. Early in the morning, when the dew is still on the grass, there is something almost worshipful in the way the scavengers encircle the hay wagons. Rusty things scrape and clink. Parked in pastures and tilted along the shoulders of the road, the trucks multiply. Expectation grows. Small talk crescendos to hubbub. The auctioneer does his sound check. The bidding begins. By noon, the atmosphere feels carnivalesque. Then, by midafternoon, a postprandial drowsiness sets in. Sun-drugged, their acquisitiveness and inquisitiveness slaked, the bidders look for places to sit—in tractor seats, on pallets of lumber, on the edges of hay wagons—and wait for the auctioneer to get around to whatever special items he is saving for last. One by one, the trucks depart.

Tom buys more tools at the Krause auction than he has at any auction so far this summer, and when it's over, after heaving several hundred pounds of junk into the back of his truck, including an enormous grinding wheel and a complete set of blacksmith's tools, we are both exhausted. Driving home, we stop at King Kone. Tom orders blackberry—not as good as orange-vanilla swirl, but good enough. While we sit at a picnic table licking melted soft-serve from our knuckles, white tufts blizzard all around us, gathering at the edges of the parking lot in drifts. I ask Tom what they are. "Cottonwood seeds," he tells me.

It is a commonplace that in the era of consumerism we are what we possess. Usually this is noted as a cause for worry, another symptom of cultural decline, and perhaps it is. Still, when you visit auctions, it is hard not to be moved to pity and awe. Gathered on lawns and hay wagons, items explain one another, like words in a language. However miscellaneous they seem, these belongings share a kind of logic—the ordering principle of human personality. One can trace among them the lineaments of an inner life. Political affiliations, religious beliefs, memories, vanities, even dreams, are spread out for strangers to browse through. Here is a man's hairpiece, here his wooden crutches, here his numismatic map of the world festooned with faded stamps. Here is the Carter-Mondale button he once wore. At another auction on another farm in another material universe, the items on offer include the October 1959 issue of *Marriage: The Magazine of Catholic Family Living,* a USDA bulletin called *Making Cellars Dry,* a miniature souvenir tool kit commemorating the Catholic shrine at Indian River, Michigan ("largest crucifix in the world"), and three framed jigsaw puzzles of pastoral scenes—sheep, glades, brooks.

Walter Benjamin blamed mechanical reproduction for diminishing the auras of unique works of art, but mass-produced artifacts also exude auras—auras created through ownership and use. They become, as Agee wrote, "images and marvels of nature." Even separated from their owners, even incoherently grouped, objects remain faintly numinous, like the relics discovered in ancient tombs. This is especially true of tools, which perhaps retain the traces of their owners more strongly than do most human artifacts.

Today we refer to anything useful, from computer programs to ideas, as tools. This was not always the case. According to Eric Sloane, in antebellum America the word "tool" denoted an implement that could make one thing at a time. Reconstruction-era industrialization broadened the meaning of the word to include any implement involved in the manufacture of a product, necessitating the coining of the term "hand tool" to distinguish traditional implements from what came to be known as "machines."

The difference between these two mechanical species, it seems to me, may be more a matter of culture than of engineering. Machines are both the rival and the antithesis of humanity. In their complexity, they resemble us. In their simplicity (all those parts, and yet no Oedipus complex, no withdrawal symptoms, no fear of death, no ecstasy), they are monstrous— or as Blake put it, "Satanic." Machines are largely autonomous and threaten us with obsolescence, whereas a tool is nothing without us.

"Considered functionally," British paleontologist Kenneth P. Oakley wrote in his influential 1949 monograph, *Man the Tool-Maker,* tools "are detachable extensions of the forelimb"— a definition that any potter, toeing his wheel, might reasonably protest. Perhaps it would be more accurate to say that tools are detachable extensions not of our forelimbs but of ourselves.

"Like the nails on a beast's paws," Eric Sloane writes, "the old tools were so much an extension of a man's hand or an added appendage to his arm, that the resulting workmanship seemed to flow directly from the body of the maker and to carry something of himself into the work." Although Sloane was an anti-unionist libertarian, on the meaning of tools he and the author of *The Communist Manifesto* agree. "Estranged from labor," writes Marx, "the laborer is self-estranged, alien to himself."

For the most serious tool aficionados, or "galoots," as

they sometimes call themselves, the hegemony of mind and machine over hand and matter entails an estrangement more profound even than the one Marx imagined, an estrangement not only from self but from time. Old tools imply an entire way of being, an artisanal cosmology. One night, lurking on a newsgroup for galoots, I come upon the following credo, posted by a woodworker named Blake Ashley:

> I refuse to be in such a hurry that I squeeze the aesthetic value out of everything to gain a few minutes of time—time which will then just be filled with more rushing and more mass-produced soul-less junk. In the drive to achieve instant gratification, we have spent a century trying to shorten the learning curve and eliminate the chance of error in every human activity. There is much good in this, but something has been almost lost in the process. The Galoots are the guardians of that which was almost lost: the challenge of trying to master a skill that can never be fully mastered, the creative freedom that comes from intimacy with a medium as complex as wood, the sense of self-sufficiency that comes from knowing that you can make a useful object with tools so simple that you can make the tools too, and the peaceful meditation of trying to bring eye, hand and wood together into harmony through finesse and understanding rather than brute force.

Old tools are relics of a mythic past, but they are also antidotes to automation, standardization, acceleration, infantilization, and to the docile brand of utopianism that holds all change to be progress.

Many of the galoots I have encountered in chat rooms and at auctions fulfill my worst expectations. Unlike other collectors, galoots can at times resemble the members of a fraternal order or a medieval guild, imagining themselves to be latter-day Knights Templar, keepers of the code, "guardians of that which was almost lost." The Mid-West Tool Collectors Association insists upon the traditional divisions of labor, consigning women and the artifacts of women's work to a special "ladies auxiliary." And the association's aging members wonder why so few men of my generation care to learn about the old tools and the old ways.

Still, uncomfortable as I am in their company, wary as I am of their nostalgia, I have begun to wonder whether they are at least partly right; maybe handiness does matter. Once upon a time, we referred to all forms of manufacturing (a Latinate word for "making by hand") as "the arts," and once upon a time all artists, manual as well as fine—masons, blacksmiths, and mechanics as well as sculptors, musicians, and poets—could find meaning in their work.

"There is something missing in our definition, vision, of a human being: the need to make," the poet Frank Bidart observed in a sequence of poems devoted to the topic of making. "The culture in which we live honors specific kinds of making (shaping or misshaping a business, a family) but does not understand how central making itself is as manifestation and mirror of the self, fundamental as eating or sleeping." The worship of old tools arises, I have begun to suspect, from the epidemic frustration of this need.

Of course, Americans still use hand tools. Although the professional crafts and trades have dwindled, the do-it-yourself market that emerged in the 1940s is large and growing. Proportionally few of us use tools skillfully anymore, but hordes of us love to play with them. We love doing it ourselves so much, in fact, that in 2003 the Stanley Works, arguably the most successful tool manufacturer in U.S. history and certainly the most iconic, sold $2.7 billion worth of tools. In July, after two months on the Michigan auction circuit, I head east to Stanley's corporate headquarters, in New Britain, Connecticut, once a capital of industry, now little more than a stagnant exurb of Hartford. Gary van Deursen, corporate vice president of innovation and design, and Carl Stoutenberg, the former company historian, now retired, have agreed to meet with me.

My route to New Britain takes me tantalizingly close to the Sloane-Stanley Museum on the banks of the Housatonic, where, atop the picturesque ruins of an iron mill, Eric Sloane's collection of edifying implements now resides. I decide to make time for the detour. According to the posted hours, the museum is open for business, but when I try the front door to the main building, I find it locked. I snoop among the deserted grounds, silent but for the crunch of my footsteps on the gravel drive. There's a flagpole with a faded flag, a few picnic tables splattered with bird droppings, an enormous tractor wheel planted like a monolith in the grass, a miniature green-and-yellow steam engine arrested in the act of pulling a miniature boxcar down a miniature section of track. Finally, a man emerges from a shed. He informs me that the tool museum is indefinitely closed due to cuts in the state budget and suggests I return when the economy improves.

Onward to New Britain. Of the dozens of manufacturers that once operated here, Stanley is the only one left. A year before my visit, CEO John Trani made national news by recommending that the toolmaker reincorporate in Bermuda. Lawmakers, labor leaders, shareholders, and New Britain residents began impugning Trani's patriotism. In the end, Stanley decided to stay put, at least on paper, at least for now. Already the company has sent most of its manufacturing jobs elsewhere (nearly 50 percent of Stanley employees work overseas) and has reduced its New Britain workforce from 5,000 fifty years ago to 1,000 today. And so, American do-it-yourselfers are buying iconic American tools made in China in order to do amateur manual labor while workers laid off by the manufacturer of those tools seek employment in the service sector.

A tall man with a grizzled mustache and a cell phone clipped to the waist of his pleated chinos, Gary van Deursen is not a galoot. He has studied and admired the tools made by his predecessors, but he thinks his are better. His great enthusiasm is industrial design—the practice of it, the idea of it, exquisite examples of it. What he designs almost doesn't seem to matter. Before joining Stanley, he worked at Black & Decker. A large poster of a DustBuster hangs on one wall of his office. He drives a blue Porsche 996 and mentions it frequently, even when he is talking about tools, as an example, a paragon, of good design. Van Deursen is goofy for Progress, gonzo for Change. Everything is getting better. And this is very exciting.

Over lunch in the corporate cafeteria, I ask van Deursen and Stoutenberg if they are familiar with Sloane's museum. "Very," Stoutenberg says, rolling his eyes.

I concede that Sloane was "a cranky guy" with strong opinions and a romantic view of the past. Still, many of the tools I've seen at tool auctions look superior—sturdier, prettier, more finely wrought—than those on sale at Home Depot. I sound, almost, like a regular galoot.

"I would use the analogy of 'the cars,'" van Deursen says. "It's easier to say that the old cars were better because they were thicker steel, but yet if you were going to have even a forty-mile-an-hour collision, what car do you want to be in? Give me any new car. And that's because of the technology that's involved."

Van Deursen begins to get excited. "Look at the measuring tape," he says in a way that reminds me of Tom Friedlander. "From the 1922 Farrand tape to the tape we made a few years ago, the end would break off after multiple retractions. In the past three years, looking at that, addressing that problem, we figured out how to solve it with technology that was invented for helicopter blades in Desert Storm. We applied clear armor made by 3M to the last six inches of the tape and increased its strength ten or twenty times."

After lunch we head to the design department, where van Deursen gives me one of these high-tech, battle-tested measuring tapes to keep as a souvenir. "PowerLock REINFORCED WITH BladeArmor 2X BLADE LIFE," the package says. This is an extreme measuring tape. This is a tape you could measure warheads and spider holes with. Packaging, I learn that afternoon, is where much of Stanley's innovation and design now occur. Even the tools themselves have been packaged, decorated, and branded with superfluous design elements—ribbed black blobs of rubber, accents of Stanley yellow—all in order to outperform the competition not in the workshop or at the construction site but at Home Depot and Wal-Mart. Functional refinements, like BladeArmor, are minor compared with the cosmetic changes the tools never-endingly undergo.

Van Deursen's job would be easier if this weren't the case— if he could simply design the best tool possible, and "best" today means safe and user-friendly as well as functional. But his customers often shop irrationally, nostalgically. In California, Stanley's framing hammer comes with a black wooden axe-handle because in California that's what house framers have traditionally used. No one at Stanley knows why. When van Deursen set out to turn Stanley's top-of-the-line chisel into an ergonomic marvel, he learned that both amateur and professional carpenters prefer chisels with translucent yellow handles, even though translucent plastic was itself a novel material only fifty years ago. As a group, tool users are late adopters. "We wanted to add rubber," van Deursen says. "We add too much rubber, and the guy isn't going to buy this, because he doesn't see his traditional material." The result is a quintessentially twenty-first-century tool, ergonomic, user-friendly, accompanied by safety precautions, made from a combination of space-age metals and polymers, including translucent yellow plastic, and exhibiting, in Van Deursen's words, "all the cues, on a global basis, of a chisel."

Just before I leave, van Deursen lets me have a sneak peek at the hot new hand tool Stanley will be rolling out in time for Christmas, the redesigned SportUtility™ Outdoorsman Knife, the name of which came to him, like inspiration from on high, while listening to a news report about SUVs. Invented to cut roofing tile and drywall, the traditional Stanley utility knife, market research showed, had become popular with hunters and fishermen. So van Deursen and his team added a three-and-a-half-inch "folding sport blade," some sporty styling, thought up a snazzy name, and doubled the suggested retail price. This

is what tools in the twenty-first century have become: not
hardware, gear.

History tends to memorialize great changes, which, techno-
logically speaking, means great inventions. Tools are inher-
ently conservative and humble artifacts. Their history is largely
accidental, written in the margins—of warfare, architecture,
economics, religion. In the history of technology, inventions
are the generals, the geniuses, the monarchs; tools are the com-
moners, the craftsmen, the serfs. This is one reason old tools
have become Americana. At once democratic and utilitarian,
individualistic and traditional, they resemble us. They are technological leaves of grass.

"Democratic nations," wrote Alexis de Tocqueville in 1831,
"will habitually prefer the useful to the beautiful and they will
want the beautiful to be useful." And tool-collecting literature
is replete with evidence of this American preference for the
useful. Eric Sloane's epigraph for *A Museum of Early American
Tools,* taken from a "tool pamphlet" written in 1719, declares
that "the Carpenter who builds a good House to defend us
from Wind and Weather, is far more serviceable than the curious Carver who employs his art to please his Fancy."

Tools are to American civilization what amphorae and
urns were to the ancient Greeks, common artifacts the ubiq-
uity and durability of which attest to their cultural importance
and ensure that they will last. Like the Grecian urn in Keats's
famous ode, they are the foster children of silence and slow
time. Long after the mills crumble into the millponds and the
cornfields sprout subdivisions, long after the sweatshops are
condemned and the machines sold off as scrap, tools remain.

"Tools outlast the worker and the work and the products," David H. Shayt, the Smithsonian Institution's specialist in crafts and trades, told me. "We can't collect people here—we even do worker's clothing very poorly—but the tool we can study and honor."

Although the history of tools is longer than that of any other human artifact, tool historians such as Shayt are comparatively novel. The first scholars to take tool-collecting seriously were Victorian archaeologists, and, like Victorian naturalists, the specimens they studied first were those from distant places and distant times. Most hoped to do for civilization what Darwin had done for life. In 1898, David Shayt's predecessors at the Smithsonian prepared a taxonomy of inventions, including musical instruments, weapons, and eating utensils as well as tools, for exhibition at the Trans-Mississippi Exposition held in Omaha, Nebraska. The first item in the exhibit's genealogy of the hammer was a quartzite pounding stone; the last, a steam-powered hammer as huge and terrible as an iron god. The published caption offers this moral: "The triumphs of human effort and ingenuity may be realized by comparing the stone hammer, still in use by half the race, with the machine hammer of today." This is also the lesson of the exhibit as a whole: Behold, the triumphs of progress. Pity your ancestors. Envy your descendants.

Many of the tools then considered highest on the evolutionary ladder—the mechanical drill, the cutter head of a planing machine, crosscut saws—are ones I've seen at auctions. Now antique and collectible, only a century ago these artifacts of the age of mechanical reproduction betokened the future, much as the quaint water wheels that ornament calendars and the bucolic suburbs of New England were in their day the very engines of change.

In 1897, a year before the Trans-Mississippi Exposition, Henry Chapman Mercer, a forty-one-year-old archaeologist from Doylestown, Pennsylvania, visited the premises of a neighbor "who had been in the habit of going to country sales and buying what they called 'penny lots.'" There, Mercer experienced a revelation of near-Pauline proportions. "When I [saw the] disordered pile of old wagons, gum-tree salt boxes, flax brakes, straw beehives, tin dinner horns, rope machines and spinning wheels, things I had heard of but never collectively saw before, the idea occurred to me that the history of Pennsylvania was here profusely illustrated." Mercer subsequently abandoned his studies of prehistory and started obsessively buying penny lots, hoping to salvage "all things illustrating the life of a people at a given time," by which he mainly meant tools, but also the objects wrought with them. In 1929 he published *Ancient Carpenters' Tools*, a novel-sized study whose encyclopedic, esoteric detail makes it only slightly less impressive than the museum Mercer constructed in Doylestown to house his 15,000 illustrious things. Since Mercer's death, with the addition of posthumous acquisitions, the collection has more than tripled.

At the recommendation of David Shayt, Carl Stoutenberg, and numerous galoots, before returning to Michigan, I decide to make what is for any serious student of American tools a necessary pilgrimage. Mercer, a practitioner as well as a historian of traditional arts and crafts, earned a fortune manufacturing Moravian tiles. Terrified of losing his collection to fire, his museum, an inflammable fortress built entirely from reinforced concrete (6,000 tons of it) and illuminated entirely by natural light (the windows comprise 5,000 panes), is intended to endure until the end of time. Witold Rybczynski, who made the pilgrimage in the late 1990s while researching *One Good Turn: A Natural History of the Screwdriver and the Screw,* aptly compares the building to "a baronial castle transplanted from the Transylvanian Alps."

Like Rybczynski, I find the experience of touring the museum dizzying. The central gallery vaults six stories to the roof, and standing at the middle of it is like standing at the bottom of a twister that has sucked the entire nineteenth century into its windy coils. Buggies, wagons, and sleighs float in midair, one above the other. A thirty-by-six-foot whaleboat hangs from the ceiling on chains. Every surface is encrusted with the antiquated remains of America's material culture. Across one wall, a trio of ox yokes fly like strange pelicans.

A walkway at the periphery of the central gallery spirals me upward past dozens of alcoves, each devoted to a different craft or trade, from wheelwrighting to glassblowing, nearly every single one of which industrialism has rendered obsolete. My favorite of the many tools I encounter on my ascent is the hatter's bow, a yard-long implement that looks just like a cellist's bow, only larger. Haberdashers would pluck the bow's taut, catgut string above a mass of loose fur, causing it, the curator's caption explains, "to interlace and produce a semi-compact, oval sheet of fibers called a 'batt.'"

On the third floor, inside a glass display case, I come upon a diagram of Mercer's taxonomy, his "Classification of Historic Human Tools," an elegant scheme that is to the Byzantine classification system devised by the U.S. Patent and Trade-

mark Office what Linnaean taxonomy is to genetic sequenc-
ing. The USPTO organizes tools first according to the action
they perform, and further according to highly particularized
nuances of engineering and design. The wrench, for instance,
belongs to Class 81 (tools), Subclass 52 (wrench, screwdriver,
or driver therefor), which contains tools "for engaging a work
part and exerting or transmitting a twisting strain thereto,
or means for imparting or transmitting an actuating force to
such a tool." Subclass 52 is in turn divided into sub-subclasses,
sub-sub-subclasses, and so on. A particular kind of Allen
wrench belongs to sub-subclass 436 (having work-engaging
and force-exerting portion inserted into cavity, e.g., Allen
wrench, screwdriver), sub-sub-subclass 442 (inserted portion
having relatively movable components), sub-sub-sub-subclass
443 (having camming or wedging element for moving components), sub-sub-sub-sub-subclass 444 (axially shiftable element located between and wedging against components), and,
finally, sub-sub-sub-sub-sub-subclass 445 (with threaded surface for cooperating with mating-tool structure).

Mercer, on the other hand, divides all human artifacts into
two kingdoms, primary and secondary, which he subsequently
organizes not formally or functionally but culturally, relativis-
tically, according to how the tool was used. Primary tools are
those used to make or procure necessities—Food, Clothing,
Shelter, Transportation, and, of course, other Tools. Secondary tools are those used in human activities less rudimentary
to survival, which Mercer groups into seven categories: Language, Religion, Commerce, Government, Art, Amusement,
and Science. For each class, primary and secondary, he offers a
single exemplary object. A tuning fork falls under Art, a pair of

spurs under Transport. A multipurpose device might belong to several different categories, depending on who used it and how. An apothecary's mortar and pestle is an artifact of Applied Science, but a baker's mortar and pestle would be an artifact of Food. The museum itself is a kind of three-dimensional, seven-story magnification of this scheme, a taxonomical honeycomb of dioramas.

It is a beautiful thing, this taxonomy, like a good, old tool, elegant and useful even today, despite its simplicity. I can think of objects that might blur Mercer's lines but none that would fall outside of them. Unlike Eric Sloane, Mercer regards objects as artifacts, not symbols. He insists that his tools not be treated as romantic, nationalistic icons, for ancient antecedents to early American tools can be found worldwide. Not only does his book include primitive examples of the wrench; he expresses disbelief that archaeologists have paid so little attention to this implement, given its importance in the history of machines.

"This singular collection is the child of an opportunity which will certainly never occur again," Mercer is quoted as saying in a display near the museum's entrance. "Let my words inspire you one and all to refrain from destroying historical specimens of this kind which happen to be in your possession." There is something poignant about this wish, poignant because the idea that one could possibly preserve the material world, make time pause, arrest "all things illustrating the life of a people at a given time," is itself antique. Mercer's elegant classification system, the vestige of a far more knowable world, contains a fatal flaw: It cannot accommodate whatsits. To classify a tool, he must first know how it was used.

For practical reasons, Mercer limited his collection to preindustrial tools. Had he included tools of the age of mechanical reproduction, he would have needed a concrete, fireproof Library of Babel to house them. Not even the Smithsonian has room for hand tools anymore. Most of the collection David Shayt curates has been moved to a warehouse in Maryland. During the last two centuries, depending on how you measure it, the manufactured world may have become even more various than the natural one, as infinite in its variety, to paraphrase Freud, as the daydreams of mankind.

Since 1790, when the U.S. Patent and Trademark Office was established, 6.7 million inventions have been patented in this country alone—more than three times the number of life forms identified to date by biologists. Of these, more than 33,000 are hand tools "not structurally limited to any classified art," a number that is itself fairly staggering when you consider that from the Iron Age to the dawn of the age of mechanical reproduction the tools of most trades remained essentially the same. The claw-headed hammer, the plane, the brace, the saw, the drill—nearly all the tools in a woodworker's toolbox predate the birth of Christ. There were good reasons for their longevity: namely, human anatomy, raw materials, and the laws of physics. A hammer swung by a Roman carpenter in 286 B.C. differed only superficially from that swung by an American in 1786 A.D. because in both cases the tool turned the carpenter's hand into a fulcrum; in both cases, the hammer's head would likely have been made of iron, and its haft from a wood such as oak, strong enough to withstand repeated shock but soft enough to conform ergonomically to the body of the man swinging it; in both cases, a well-aimed blow would have delivered comparable force and an errant one comparable harm.

With the emergence of machine lathes and modern metallurgy at the turn of the nineteenth century, it suddenly became possible to mass-produce tools so specialized they could substitute for skills. "The productivity of labour depends not only on the proficiency of the worker, but also on the quality of his tools," Karl Marx wrote in a section of *Das Kapital*, "The Specialized Worker and His Tools." By 1867, Marx reports with a hint of surprise and dismay, five hundred different varieties of hammer were being manufactured in Birmingham, England. Flip through *The Hammer: The King of Tools*, a collector's field guide; behold the fabulous, many-headed throng pictured therein—snow knockers and hoof picks, thrifts and mauls, stonecutting hammers with polls like picket fences, commanders with massive heads of burl, fencing hammers with "wire twisting cheeks"—and you can appreciate Marx's astonishment.

The same year Marx published *Das Kapital*, the number of U.S. patents totaled 60,658, an increase in three decades of more than 5,000 percent. In 1928, the year Mercer completed *Ancient Carpenters' Tools*, Americans patented 42,376 inventions, and in 1930, at the beginning of the Great Depression, they patented not fewer but more—45,243 in all. This is because patents exist in the realm of fantasy, not in the realm of market economics. They represent the American dream in its purest, most lottery-like form. Of course, many if not most patented inventions never earn a dime, and a majority of those that do quickly become extinct. Proof of this technological mass extinction is all around us. In fields and barns, foreclosed factories and abandoned mines, in plastic buckets of melted hail, the Bessemer age of mechanical reproduction is vanishing into rust. For this reason, the database of the U.S. Patent and Trademark Office, like Tom Friedlander's barn, resembles both a cabinet of wonders and a catacomb of follies.

What Mercer's museum most reminds me of is Oxford University's natural history museum, a cathedral-like building crowded with display cases. American museums of natural history, with their animatronic dinosaurs, IMAX screens, and laserized planetarium shows, increasingly resemble amusement parks. The Oxford museum, by comparison, has the feel of a postcolonial curiosity shop, as if the curators had wandered amid the wreckage of the British Empire, scavenging haphazardly whatever marvels and oddities they could find. Walking from display case to display case, one skips across continents and centuries. Here is the foot of a dodo bird, here the shriveled head of a pygmy, here the plaster-of-paris likeness of an Iguanodon.

There is something funereal about all natural history museums. They are zoos of the dead, not only because they exhibit herds of skeletons and flocks of stuffed birds but because so many of their specimens are extinct. On one of my scavenger hunts with Tom, I picked up a battered copy of Darwin's *Journal of Researches* and, reading it, was struck by how anachronistic—how innocent, even—his exuberant curiosity seemed. His entries are rhapsodies of descriptive prose. Forms of the words "interesting" and "surprising" toll among his sentences like a refrain of wonderment. "I was much surprised to find particles of stone above the thousandth of an inch square, mixed with finer matter," he writes of a handful of dust. It is as if no one in the history of the world had ever paid attention before, as if Darwin and other Victorians had been born at the dawn of creation, rather than at the twilight of an empire.

For Melville, too, the seas were a sublime chaos of Leviathan mysteries—mysteries that, in a famously dense chapter on "Cetology," Ishmael endeavors to solve, wielding taxonomy as deftly as Queequeg does a harpoon. Although he "swam through libraries and sailed through oceans," a systematic classification of the whale, he concedes, would take generations to complete. Never could Melville have predicted that within seventy-five years of *Moby-Dick*'s publication, when the last American whaling bark, *Wanderer,* sank off Cuttyhunk, not only would all the species of the once-unfathomable cetacean order have been fathomed but many would be nearly extinct and the whale fisheries nearly exhausted. One wonders to what degree Darwin, Melville, and other taxonomical Victorians realized that their travelogues were eulogies.

Upon my return to Michigan, I decide to take one last field trip into the American junkyard. For five days in late August, the thirty-eighth annual Tri-State Gas Engine & Tractor Show will be held at the Jay County fairgrounds in Portland, Indiana. Hundreds of tool dealers will be in attendance. To get a jump on other collectors, Tom drives down ahead of time and spends the eve of the show in a motel. I arrive the following morning a little before noon. The dirt parking lots reserved for the show are nearly full. Throughout the surrounding neighborhood, people are renting out parking spots on their front lawns. The cars, hailing from across the Midwest, may very well number in the thousands.

Imagining that Tom's blue cap and long beard will make him easy to spot, I procure a map and head to the section of the grounds labeled ANTIQUES. Among the tables of John Deere memorabilia and hand-painted weathervanes, I find a few tool dealers, but Tom is nowhere to be seen. I wander the grounds, past concession stands peddling corn dogs and fried dough, and septuagenarian blacksmiths demonstrating their lost art. On and on I search, up and down the seemingly endless rows of gas engines and tractors, whose proud owners sit beside them in folding chairs, drinking beer and playing cards. A hundred years ago, these antique machines, nearly all of them now lovingly restored, brought industry to the farm. They are, in effect, factories on wheels. Passover is thought to have begun as a shepherds' feast, the rituals and symbols of which outlasted the way of life that gave rise to them. Something similar, it seems to me, is happening here, at this celebration of obsolete technology. Caravanning multitudes have made the pilgrimage in order to sacrifice a few gallons of fossil fuel to the Gods of Industry. Out of the smokestack of a Leviathan diesel mill with a flywheel weighing three tons, perfect rings of smoke chuff one by one at rhythmic intervals, expanding as they rise.

The day is well past its meridian when I realize that the Jay County fairgrounds are far larger than I had thought. In one corner of my map, north of the spark-plug exhibit and east of the tractors, the word "parts" appears twice, adrift in a terra incognita of white space. Here, in a vast and shadeless field, I discover a postindustrial bazaar. The place feels like a makeshift village or the camp of a bivouacking army. Booths and tables, overspread with mechanical organs and implements, form thoroughfares several acres long.

There are dealers who specialize in antique spark plugs, antique railroad jacks, antique wooden pulleys, antique hog oilers, antique tractor-seat cushions. There is even a magazine stand peddling such periodicals as *Green,* a John Deere fanzine, and *Farm Collector* ("Dedicated to the Preservation of Vintage Farm Equipment"). When I finally locate Tom, he is standing alone at a Coca-Cola kiosk, tinted shades clipped to his glasses, two duffle bags at his feet, both bulging with loot. Since not long after sunrise, he has been working his way from dealer to dealer, filling his bags and returning to his truck to empty them. He has already acquired more wrenches on this hunt than on any other in all his years of collecting, and he still has a few more dealers he means to hit before we go.

The next day, back in Michigan, I drive out to the Friedlanders' farm to help Tom unload, tally, and classify this bounteous haul. Spreading his treasures out on the lowered tailgate of his pickup, he is boyishly giddy. "Whee!" he sings. "Christmas in August!" Today the world delights him with surprises. A wasp swoops down from the eaves of the tool barn, snatches a grasshopper from the dirt, and carries it away. "Grasshopper killer!" Tom exclaims. It is a perfect late-summer afternoon. The cattails have grown as tall as trees. Martha's vegetable garden is in fruit. The light is golden. The goldenrod is a yellow sea. The grass beside the tool barn is long and spangled with dandelions. Among them, I notice first one little Day-Glo orange flag, then another, then another. There are four in all.

"That's where the new barn will go," Tom explains when I ask about the flags. The new barn has been a fantasy of his for years. At last, he is ready to build it. As we sort yesterday's quarry into piles—wrenches here, nonwrenches there, hand-forged wrenches there, drop-forged wrenches here—Tom describes his plans. The new barn will be bigger than the last barn, he says, and more brightly lit—an exhibition space worthy of his collection. He will mount his tools on plywood and hang them from walls. I wonder who it is he imagines his museum will attract, or if it even matters. As much as he enjoys my interest in his tools, I doubt that his excitement would diminish if I weren't there. If he were his museum's only patron, I am certain that he would keep rescuing tools, keep classifying them, keep putting them on display. Identification is, for him, akin to benediction, and salvage is akin to salvation. His cosmology, I have come to learn, is essentially elegiac. The universe he inhabits is at once wondrous and endangered. He is not a religious man. He does not believe that The End is nigh. Trained as a botanist, he does not believe in The End at all but in evolution, change without end. And yet, unlike some neo-Darwinists, Tom knows that change entails loss, and he does not confuse evolution with progress.

That afternoon, when we have finished archiving Tom's new acquisitions, I linger in the barn, alone. Outside, the world is hot and bright, but inside it is cool and dark. It smells of grease, dirt, concrete, rust. There are no windows. One might as well be underground, in a cave—or in a dream. The shapes of the tools are fabulous, as is their multiplicity, and their glimmering is faintly sentient, like the eyes of dolls.

I choose an item at random and take notes. Copper-headed hammer, nine-inch handle made of tapered iron. No maker's mark, no patent number. One poll cracked, the other poll scurfy with blue-green oxides that come off, like butterfly scales, when you touch them. Copper mines riddle northern Michigan and southern Ontario, on land stolen from natives

for its ore. Now many of the mines are depleted, and the copper, at least a small part of it, is dissolving onto my fingertips.

In the first chapter of *Democracy in America*, de Tocqueville
characterized the European settlers of the American Midwest
as "the great people to whom the future of the continent doubt-
less belongs." No longer. The future lies elsewhere now, in suburban business parks, in the coastal metropolises, or perhaps
on another continent altogether. Perhaps the future belongs to
the employees of Stanley's factory in China.

Today the residents of "that inexhaustible Mississippi Valley" resemble those other peoples de Tocqueville describes
in his first chapter, a mysterious, vanished, and—as history
would later prove—wholly imaginary tribe who allegedly preceded the Indians. "Along the banks of the Ohio and in all of
the central valley," de Tocqueville wrote, "every day one still
finds mounds raised by the hand of man. When one digs to the
center of these monuments, they say, one can scarcely fail to
encounter human remains, strange instruments, arms, utensils
of all kinds—made of metal, or recalling usages unknown to
current races."

Like a rusty, obsolete machine that was once as silvery and
marvelous as the future itself, the New World, that European
pipe dream, has grown old. This is one of the meanings I have
scavenged from the junkyard.

"Democratic peoples scarcely worry about what has been,"
de Tocqueville also wrote, "but they willingly dream of what
will be, and in this direction their imagination has no limits;
here it stretches and enlarges itself beyond measure." To the
degree that this was ever true—and the suicidal immigrants
in Willa Cather's novels present at least one caveat—I doubt it

is any longer. At some point in the 175 years that have elapsed since the French aristocrat came to have a look at the American experiment in democracy—perhaps when the frontier closed, or perhaps when men became, in Thoreau's words, "the tools of their tools," or perhaps when Henry C. Mercer acquired his first penny lot—the future loosened its purchase upon our dreams. This is not to say that Americans have collectively lost faith in progress, only that our imaginations face in two directions. Newer is still better, but now we are nostalgic for almost everything.

REVIVAL OF THE ICE CANOE

A half hour to race time, the snow still coming down, Jean Anderson had a decision to make: canoe number 79, or 181. Number 181 was new, state of the art, the best canoe Anderson had engineered. Whereas 79 was a warhorse, banged up by ice, dented, punctured, patched. What made Anderson's decision difficult was the snow. So much was coming down that, from the frozen edge of Bassin Louise, you could barely make out the Saint Lawrence's far shore. On the river's gray surface, a puzzling pack of ice floes drifted south, headed upstream, the way they'd come.

Here, at Quebec City, approaching the gulf with which it shares a name, the Saint Lawrence River falls under the tidal influence of the North Atlantic. A half hour before race time, the tides were nearing full flood, turning the river back. If you were used to rivers that flow downstream, and downstream only, the upstream floes were a strange sight, as if the river were rewinding itself.

Bassin Louise is a marina on Quebec City's waterfront. In the summer, pleasure boats come and go from the docks there, traveling downstream to the North Atlantic, or upstream via the Saint Lawrence Seaway to the Great Lakes. The upstream boats go where canoes used to—Toronto, Detroit, Chicago, Duluth.

In winter, Bassin Louise freezes over, solidly enough near shore that you probably could do donuts on it in a monster truck if you wanted to. One weekend every winter, the docks wake up from their hibernation. Way out on the basin's frozen center, a portable generator inflates a pneumatic finish line, turning it first into an angry rubber anaconda and then into a plump arch.

A few hundred athletes clad in crampons, nylon, and neoprene, as if for some special operation, descend aluminum gangways. On the gangways, their crampons clatter. On the ice, they click. A stevedore's crane lowers colorful canoes one by one onto the ice, as if depositing sashimi onto a plate.

The canoes aren't ordinary canoes. They're ice canoes, built and painted to race, according to specifications issued by the officials in charge of the competitive ice-canoe circuit: twenty-eight feet long, at least four at the beam. Made of carbon fiber and Kevlar and epoxy, they are almost as long and about as wide as the 600-pound wooden maître-class beasts in which voyageurs and fur traders used to travel the Saint Lawrence, but much lighter, around 250 pounds. In place of thwarts, most ice canoes have seats that slide on rails like the seats of sculls. Each canoe carries five paddlers—*canotiers*, the paddlers of canoes are called in Quebec. Only the *barreur*, French for "helmsman" or "coxswain," actually paddles with a paddle. The other four canotiers pull on oars modified from those used in Olympic rowing, which technically makes canotiers rowers, not paddlers. Ice-canoe oars have ice picks soldered to their blades—they resemble railroad stakes, big nails—because sometimes canotiers are rowing through water and sometimes they are rowing through pack ice. Most but not all ice canoes have paint jobs favoring colors—orange, red, yellow—that are easy to see amid the gray and white welter of water and floes and falling snow. Alongside racing numbers, their hulls advertise the names of sponsors: a pub, the Quebec City Police Department, banks, hotels, an automaker, a law firm, a cheesemonger.

A half hour before race time, the voices of the sportscasters alternated with pop songs, blasting through loudspeakers positioned along the balustrade, excited patter and excited chords bouncing off the riprap and the ice and the concrete walls of Bassin Louise. On the pier, a large crowd huddled and stamped their feet to stay warm while waiting for the race—the oldest and grandest on the competitive ice-canoe circuit—to begin. The cold was a draw more than a deterrent; Quebec is the birthplace of ice canoeing—or, as it's called in French, *canot à glace*—and Quebec City's annual ice-canoe race is the Kentucky Derby, the Grand Prix, or, as one of the sportscasters put it on that February morning, "le Super Bowl" of *canot à glace*. On the frozen basin, carrying a clipboard, a race official walked among the turtled canoes dusted with snow, inspecting them. Out on the Saint Lawrence, a tremendous freighter, blue hull streaked with rust, was steaming south, blocks of ice tumbling before its prow.

Ice canoeing is to Quebec something like what surfing is to Hawaii, except that, unlike the surfboard—or the bark canoe, for that matter—the ice canoe has yet to attract many enthusiasts beyond its place of origin. Odds are, it never will. It evolved over the course of centuries in response to the peculiar conditions of the Lower Saint Lawrence. Upstream from Quebec City, before the arrival of steamboats, the river froze into a reliable ice road. People living near what is now Montreal traveled the river by snowshoe or dogsled, later by horse. But in Quebec City, most winter months, the brackish tides kept open a channel, down which, riding the ebb and the flood, drifted a shifting labyrinth of floes. If for some dire reason you needed to enter that labyrinth, and hoped to exit it, you had little choice but to take a canoe.

Canoes had a distinct advantage over heavier boats: In theory at least, beset paddlers could portage over the ice—climbing out onto the slippery, tippy, drifting platform of a floe, dragging their canoe to open water. These midstream portages often proved to be as perilous as you'd expect. The French colonists who settled Quebec in the sixteenth century picked up the practice from the Algonquin Indians who'd preceded them. You can find in colonial journals and memoirs accounts of canoes crushed by ice, of drownings, of castaways stranded on floes.

By the nineteenth century, wooden canoes had replaced bark canoes and ice canoeing had become a profession. Canotiers were the teamsters and taxi drivers of the Lower Saint Lawrence, connecting Quebec City with settlements on the river's south bank, or on the islands downstream. There are old photographs and paintings of canotiers transporting bundles of mail or paying passengers—men in dark suits, women in fur coats—across jagged fields of ice. Students who lived in Lévis, Quebec City's outer borough, on the south bank, would commute by ice canoe. So would doctors and priests.

The arrival of steamboats and bridges made ice canoes and canotiers, practically speaking, obsolete, but like other obsolete modes of transportation (horses, sailboats, kayaks, bark canoes), ice canoes found a second life as pastime and sport, and in Quebec, if nowhere else, that sport is increasingly popular and increasingly competitive.

Along with an obsolete mode of transportation, ice canoe races have preserved anachronistic knowledge—knowledge older than North America's recorded history. Those of us who live south of the Canadian border tend to forget how much of our own early history was written in French. The territory Jefferson purchased from Napoleon was in fact a mere remnant of the realm the French had claimed more than a century before in the name of Louis XIV. At its inception, Louisiana had encompassed the entirety of the Mississippi Basin—stretching from the Rockies in the West to the Appalachians in the East. Mississippi does not mean "Father of Waters," as you might have heard. It's the phonetic spelling of what the Algonquian for "Big River" sounded like to some Frenchman's ears. *Miss* is in fact the same Algonquian word as the *Mich* in Michigan, which is the phonetic spelling of what an Algonquian phrase, meaning "Big Water," sounded like to some other Frenchman.

Forget the wagon trains, Manifest Destiny, the frontier receding westward across the continent. Long before the arrival of Europeans and for a few centuries after, people traveled through the American interior by canoe, plying a vascular system of water routes that meandered and branched in all four of the cardinal directions, connecting the Great Lakes to the Mississippi, the Gulf of Saint Lawrence to the Gulf of Mexico.

From Quebec, a voyageur could paddle all the way to Lake Superior, or farther. Two decades before people in Salem started hunting witches, Frenchmen in canoes had already visited the wondrous and populous realm called Peoria. Most of those first documented expeditions into the region now known ingloriously as the American Midwest—or sentimentally as the Heartland, or dismissively as Flyover Country—had begun and ended on the Lower Saint Lawrence.

I'd driven to Quebec City in a banged-up warhorse of a station wagon, traveling icy highways that approximated the old water routes, skirting the Canadian coasts of Lakes Erie and Ontario, following the Saint Lawrence north. A trip that by canoe would have taken six weeks, by station wagon had taken twelve hours. But speed had come at a cost. Our mobility had blurred away a finer-scale geography—a subtler sense of place. However useless and anachronistic, the knowledge canotiers had preserved, acquired, and passed down by generations seemed to me worth saving.

In an essay on rivers, poet Robert Hass writes that "[t]hough the names are still magic—Amazon, Congo, Mississippi, Niger, Plate, Volga, Tiber, Seine, Ganges, Mekon, Rhine, Colorado, Marne, Orinoco, Rio Grande—the rivers themselves have almost disappeared from consciousness in the modern world. Insofar as they exist in our imagination, that existence is nostalgic." To that disappearance, that nostalgia, canotiers had found—or so I'd hoped—one antidote.

~

Jean Anderson's team, Team Château Frontenac—named for its chief sponsor, the luxury hotel that is Quebec's most famous landmark—was favored to win the day's race, and the following week's in Montreal, and all nine races on the 2017 circuit. They win the Quebec City race so often that every year, in anticipation, the staff of Château Frontenac arranges a postrace victory celebration—sometimes attended by hundreds—in the hotel's banquet hall. Since forming his own team in 1985, Anderson had won the circuit twenty-six times, more than any other team captain in the sport's history. "He's like the Tiger Woods of ice canoeing," a former teammate, Eric Fraser, told me, which may not sound as glamorous or as remunerative as being the Tiger Woods of golf, but in Quebec, Anderson is legendary.

He does have a pair of long-standing rivals—the Brothers Gilbert, Guy and Yves. Yves, the eldest member of Team Volvo, is known to his teammates as *Le Vulcan*, the Vulcan—not, mind you, because he outwardly resembles the awkward-eared positivists of *Star Trek,* but because his teammates have concluded, judging by his refusal to wear a hat in abhorrently cold weather, steam radiating off his head into the subzero air, that "he's probably from another planet." Anderson had learned the sport from the Brothers Gilbert before leaving to start his own team. Together the Gilberts and Anderson are widely credited with turning ice-canoe races from an old-timey celebration of Quebecois culture and history into a borderline-professional sporting event that you could almost imagine at the Olympics, if only there were more rivers on the planet like the Saint Lawrence. At the big Quebec City race in 2000, just eighteen teams competed. By 2017, that number had risen to fifty-eight.

Balding and bespectacled, Anderson has a physique more suggestive of a scarecrow than an Olympian, but he trains hard year-round, in summer months trading a canoe for a ten-speed. Quebecois accents vary from county to county. Anderson's is so strong that to my unaccustomed ears he might as well have been speaking Portuguese. We communicated—in a mixture of French and English—mostly through Anderson's longtime teammate, Michel Lessard. Anderson and Lessard, both engineers, run a factory that makes equipment for technical schools. Students around the world learn to repair wind turbines and air conditioners on equipment the factory makes. At one end of the factory floor, in a space the size of an airplane hangar, under mysterious hooks running along mysterious conveyances, Anderson and Lessard have set up what they call "the laboratory," where they conduct ice-canoe R&D.

Since the early 1980s, when fiberglass boatmaking became affordable, canotiers have been experimenting with the canoe, molding—first out of fiberglass, later out of carbon fiber— novel hull shapes more hydrodynamic than the traditional ones permitted by bark or wood. Their inventors tend to name these designs after sea creatures found in the waters off Quebec. The varieties of ice canoe now include the Beluga, the Sardine, the Narwhal, the Orca. Anderson has invented the two canoes— the Capelin, named for a species of fish, and the Dolphin—that have in recent years become the sport's standard.

Their younger teammates refer to Lessard and Anderson as "the old men"—*les vieux*. They take no offense. They are old enough, in their late fifties, though you wouldn't know it, watching them hauling away on the oars. When they retire, they plan to paddle across the Arctic with a team of men and dogs. "We want to make a special canoe," Lessard told me. "You can turn the canoe over, make it a house. You'll be able to go across ice in it, with dogs. Ice, water; ice, water." Competing on the ice-canoe circuit is their way of training for this Arctic passage. One of the younger members of their team has an Olympic gold medal in speed skating, another is a firefighter who works in subarctic mines. Another works as a physical trainer for the Canadian military. What *les vieux* bring to the team is experience, expertise, and above all an obsessive technological perfectionism, which explained why, a half hour before race time, they were still deciding which canoe to race.

All the other ice canoes on the frozen basin were easily distinguished by their logos and paint jobs, but canoes 79 and 181 were an identical glossy shade of construction-cone orange. If not for their racing numbers, you would have had a hard time telling them apart. Team Château Frontenac was the only team that had brought two canoes to the starting line instead of one. Back at their laboratory, Anderson and Lessard had applied a different wax treatment to each—a different mixture of waxes, spread out in different thicknesses in different places. Their wax recipes are top secret. To understand their secrecy, and the importance of wax, you have to understand that an ice canoe, even more than most canoes, is an amphibious vehicle—half sled, half boat. Along the keel there runs a polished strip that on ice acts as an enormous skate, on snow as an enormous ski.

In any canoe race on any river or stream, paddlers have to gauge the currents. In an ice-canoe race they also have to gauge the ice. On the Saint Lawrence, the pack ice shifts and reshuffles itself from minute to minute. You'll see a channel of open water and aim for it, performing geometry in your head, calculating your speed, compensating for the current, and then, as you draw near, the wind will gust, the ice pack will change course, the channel will close up, and you'll find yourself faced with no choice but to make a transition—the deceptively bland term for a complicated feat of waterborne gymnastics that is perhaps the hardest element for rookies to master.

When the canoe's prow grinds onto a floe, the canotiers

unsnap their long oars from the oarlocks, stow them—taking care not to skewer each other with the ice picks soldered to the oar blades—then leap from their seats onto the gunwales, balancing there for a second on their knees before, with a little spin, dropping one shin into a padded brace bolted to the inner wall of the tumble home. They throw the other leg overboard and commence to scoot. That's the term for it, even in Canadian French—scooting, or sometimes scootering. To scoot, you kick at the ice, propelling the canoe as if launching a bobsled, except that unlike bobsledders, canotiers rarely scoot with two feet, rarely place their full weight on the ice, which can give way without warning. Even still, it is not uncommon for canotiers to take a hypothermic dip. Sometimes the canotiers to starboard are scooting on ice while those to port are kicking through water or slush. When floes collide, they saw at each other. Fragments pile up. After repeated collisions, the fragments build into jagged breastworks, little Himalayan ranges of ice, over which the canotiers have to wrangle their boats. Reaching open water, they perform another transition, spin back into their sliding seats, and take up their oars.

Scooting explains why canotiers sheathe their legs in shin guards and neoprene, and why they wear crampons or cleats. The members of Team Château Frontenac have scars on their legs where they took a teammate's cleat to the thigh. On scrappier teams, canotiers will screw sawed-off bolts into the soles of rugby shoes. With their characteristic perfectionism, the canotiers on Anderson's team wear, over neoprene booties, expensive artisanal crampons made to order by a manufacturer of medical prosthetics.

"A race like this, you win on scooting," Lessard told me. "It's very rare that you win it with paddling. Because with paddling there's no great difference between two teams. You are very strong, or not strong. It's about the same speed: twelve kilometers an hour compared to eleven." On the ice, a team skilled at transitions and scooting can maintain some forward momentum even while surmounting obstacles. At their fastest, Anderson's team can average a scooting speed of six, seven, maybe eight kilometers an hour. Teams that have strength but poor technique flounder on the ice.

You have to know how to read the ice, Lessard told me, and you have to know, before race time, how to wax your canoe. The wax job can decide a race. The treatment Anderson and Lessard had applied to canoe 181 was optimal for dry and icy conditions. Canoe 79 had been waxed for snow, which under humid conditions adheres like glue. They'd planned to race 181, the newer of the two, but now they were reconsidering. They'd taken 181 out on the river and hadn't liked the feel of it. Too much snow. It was supposed to let up but showed no sign of doing so.

Before the race, snow still falling, the team assembled in the back of Lessard's minivan to power up on jelly sandwiches and strategize. There followed a flurry of French, from which I snatched phrases. I kept hearing the word *tabernac*, which literally means tabernacle, but Quebecois slang has poetically transformed the vocabulary of the Catholic Church into expressive blasphemies. Tabernac, somehow, has acquired the percussive potency of an F-bomb.

Lessard would be the barreur today, which meant he would be sitting astern in the coxswain's seat, navigating the course, calling out commands to his teammates, who would all be seated facing him, backs turned to whatever surprises lay ahead, pulling on their oars in synchrony, listening to Lessard, who, when he saw ice to the left, would shout out, "*Babord-ba!*" or if to the right, "*Tribord-ti!*" *Babord* and *tribord* are French for "port" and "starboard." Because the ice can be deafening, and because *babord* and *tribord* end in the same syllable, the barreur appends an extra syllable to each, *ba* and *ti*, making them easier to distinguish. If there were ice straight ahead, Lessard would shout, "Up *en avant!*" and then "Scoot, scoot, scoot." Today, Anderson would assume the role of ice captain—a confusing term, since the barreur is mostly in charge, except midscoot. The ice captain sits up front in the bow. When scooting, afforded the best view of the terrain ahead, he takes command. Anderson, who is tall (six feet and change), often plays this role because when a canoe is surmounting a ridge of ice, the prow will shoot up into the air, and, standing on a floe, the ice captain has to reach up and wrestle the canoe back down.

"You'll need total vigilance," Lessard told the team now, in his minivan. "But you also must be relaxed. No crying out. No games. Keep your sangfroid! No emotions!" By the time they emerged from the minivan into the heavy snow, Anderson and Lessard had settled on canoe 79. An hour later, it was 181 they brought to the starting line.

Five minutes to race time, the sportscasters called for a moment of silence. The loudspeakers quieted, as did the crowd. A week before, at a local mosque, a terrorist had gunned down six worshipers. Over Bassin Louise there settled a stillness. On the pier, pressed against the cold railing among many strangers, you could hear the rustle of Gore-Tex and nylon. You could almost hear the snow. All that seemed to move was the ice, headed upstream.

And then, with a blast, the silence ended and the race began.

Whether spectators or competitors, what else do we seek from sport, other than to slow time down and give it a more discernible shape—marked, say, by a starting line and a finish line, divided into laps, reducing history to moments because moments are easier to understand and abide? A race intensifies time, and by intensifying it, a race banishes for its brief duration, or attempts to, both the future and the past.

This is how an ice-canoe race begins: madly, with a cumbersome yet agile dash, a burst of scooting, the teams pushing their canoes across the land-fast ice to the river's edge, trying to build momentum. When canotiers are scooting, their canoes look a bit like beetles with five legs. Heard from the pier, the noise of canoes on ice was reminiscent of the sound a skate's blade makes on ice, or a skateboard's axle on a curb. Heard from within the canoe, the noise is thunderous. The team that reaches the river first has the advantage of picking their course, but there are advantages to following behind: You can let the team ahead plow your path.

Team Volvo took the early lead, reaching the water's edge several seconds ahead of Team Château Frontenac, which was vying for third place. Jean Anderson had chosen to hug the southern wall of Bassin Louise. Team Volvo—in a royal-blue canoe, the automaker's name written in white block letters along its sides—had shot straight down the middle. Today, the team did not include the Vulcan, though it would the following week in Montreal. Instead, the pilot seat was occupied by Yves and Guy Gilbert's nephew, Benoit Gilbert. Volvo's blue canoe nosed from the basin into the water. The canotiers transitioned just in time, leaping in, and rowed a few strokes. A dozen yards out, they entered the ice pack and transitioned again. Scooting, they aimed for the southeastern shore while the drifting ice carried them southwest.

The tides are what make Quebec City's race, in most years, among the least predictable of the seven races on the ice-canoe circuit. The push and pull between river and tide, between brackish water and fresh, creates fluid dynamics more chaotic than you'll find elsewhere on the Saint Lawrence, or on most rivers. The river bends at Quebec. Confronted by an incoming tide, the downstream current—succumbing to the Coriolis force—favors the far, southern shore. The incoming tide favors the northern shore near Quebec City. The two together—current and tide—set the river's surface spinning.

The ice midstream, Eric Fraser told me, resembles "turntables." Michel Lessard described an ice-canoe race as "two dimensional," by which he meant that unlike other races, there is no track or lane to follow. The course is a shape-shifting terrain. The possibilities before you are ever-changing. You have to triangulate to make it through the turntables.

Say you're midstream. Say you're Lessard. In the helmsman's seat. Of canoe 181. Languishing in third place. Wondering if perhaps you and Jean Anderson have chosen the wrong canoe but also trying to banish that thought along with all other distractions. You are trying to read the ice ahead, trying to pick your course through it. At the same time, because the turntables are spinning, you have to keep glancing behind you, toward the way you came, to the north shore, where from the river's edge Quebec City ascends to the red-brick towers of Château Frontenac. On the north shore you've picked two points. Maybe point one is Château Frontenac, high atop the bluff. Maybe point two is the long column of giant concrete silos at the grain terminal beside the docks of Bassin Louise. While keeping your eye on your two points, you also keep your eye on the target across the river. And on the intervening ice. And on the blue canoe of Team Volvo.

Quebec City was built at a defensible bottleneck. The city's name is a French transliteration of *kébec*, Algonquian for "where the river narrows." When the river reverses, the bottleneck clogs with floes. There's a lake a hundred miles upstream, about halfway to Montreal, a swelling in the river, Lake Saint Pierre, that marks the terminus of the influence of the tides. In the spring, when the lake's ice breaks up, floes drifting past Quebec City sometimes carry traces of the lives lived upstream: the tracks of snowmobiles, folding chairs, a fishing hut. These traces will travel along the city's waterfront, heading north. They'll return on the incoming tide, heading south, then return once more when the tide goes out. Finally, they will disappear from view, bound for the sea, where the ice will eventually melt, casting its cargo adrift or letting it sink.

Next week's race upstream in Montreal would be comparatively tame. Ship traffic long ago obliterated Montreal's ice road. The river is as narrow there as it is at Quebec City, but at Montreal, the river behaves the way rivers usually behave, flowing in one direction, carrying the ice downstream. Here at Quebec, you have to study the tidal charts, and plan your race accordingly, minimizing the time you spend on what canotiers call *le tapis roulant*, French for "treadmill." Literally: "the rolling rug." Caught on the treadmill, rowing against a current, a weak team will stall. The more time on the treadmill, the longer your race; the less time, the shorter. Back in the minivan, Lessard and Anderson had told their teammates to save some strength for the final leg of every lap. They'd need to power through the tide.

Ten minutes after the elite men launched, the elite women followed, scooting across the ice, plowing ruts that fanned out from the starting line. Finally, ten minutes later, came the hoi polloi, the thirty-eight teams of the sport division, some plowing new ruts, most availing themselves of the ruts already plowed. At the prow of the team sponsored by the Quebec Police Department, a red siren silently spun.

It took the elite men around forty-five minutes to complete a single lap, and for much of that time, they were upstream, out of view. The spectators were left to wonder and wait, shivering on the pier. French colonists, ignorant of the Gulf Stream and its effect on Europe's weather, were baffled by Canada's frigid climate. Quebec City, after all, occupies the same approximate latitude as Bordeaux. In 1684, a French military officer, the Baron of Lahontan, arrived in the colony identified on maps as New France. Winter there was so cold, Lahontan wrote in a letter home, that "one ought to have his Blood compos'd of Brandy, his Body of Brass, and his Eyes of Glass."

Team Château Frontenac returned to the basin alone, completing the first lap three minutes ahead of Team Volvo. The rest of the elite men were languishing out of view. Frontenac's lead seemed to fulfill the prophecies of oddsmakers. No way could anyone close a lead like that. But then the unexpected happened. Château Frontenac and Team Volvo completed their second lap just as canoes in the sport division were completing their first. Turning onto the final leg, Lessard, piloting canoe 181, found himself confronted with a choice: paddle up a watery channel crowded with canoes, or circumvent the crowd by scootering over ice sticky with snow. He chose the ice.

In the pilot seat of Volvo's blue canoe, Benoit Gilbert chose the crowd—the riskier choice, since unskilled teams in the sport division can behave haphazardly. Hemmed in against the waterfront's wall, there'd be little room to maneuver. Sure enough, a collision occurred, violent enough to snap one of Team Volvo's four oars. This handicap should have knocked them out, but as it so happened, Gilbert had brought with him a kayak paddle that he'd recently been experimenting with on open water. His teammates passed it to the canotier up front, and they kept going, two oars to starboard, one oar to port, a canoe paddle in back, a kayak paddle at the bow. Rowing and paddling, dodging and weaving through the flotilla of canoes, even with a broken oar, Volvo made better time than Frontenac did on the sticky ice.

Frontenac held the lead all the way back to the target to the left of the finish line, but barely. Beginning the third and final lap, scooting across the frozen surface of Bassin Louise, the two teams hit the water and then the ice pack only seconds apart, executing their transitions almost in unison. All the way across the river, they paced each other, reaching the far shore at precisely the same moment, crossing oars as they fought to touch the target, and by the time the blue canoe and the orange one disappeared from view, upstream, around the bend, the race was a dead heat.

During my time in Quebec, I did manage to learn firsthand what it's like out there, in the labyrinth of floes, freezing your ass off while attempting to perform waterborne gymnastics. There's an outfitter that for a couple hundred bucks will set you up with an ice canoe and a seasoned canotier or two to serve as guides.

After a brief onshore tutorial, we went charging down the riverbank through deep snow, pushing a sky-blue carbon-fiber Dolphin before us. I am not by nature agile. Nor am I particularly athletic. I do paddle, but only in spring and summer, and only recreationally, and mostly on the exurban lakes and streams of southeast Michigan, rather docile bodies of water whereon sunbathers like to float in inner tubes outfitted sidecar-style with coolers of beer.

By the time we reached the edge of the landfast ice and prepared to take the plunge, I was already winded, but our barreur, an environmental cartographer named Marie-Janick Robitaille, proved to be a pitiless commander—a joyful one, but pitiless.

The tide was just beginning to come in. We rowed against it, heading north by northeast, downstream. Near our launch site, an icebreaker lay at anchor, and I kept glancing at its huge red hull, hoping to see it shrink into the distance, which it did, but far more slowly than I'd have liked. "To the right!" Robitaille shouted in English, and I lifted my oar blade to clear a passing floe. In those instances when you didn't clear your blade in time, the ice could pin the oar handle against your chest. To escape you had to yank it from the oarlock, liberate the blade, then slam the oar back into place. To a skilled canotier, this rarely happened. To me, it happened many times.

"Ready up front!" Robitaille shouted, and up front, the canotiers prepared to execute a transition. I kept rowing, sustaining the canoe's momentum as it beached upon a floe. "Ready in back!" Robitaille shouted. I wasn't, but I faked it. It is difficult, I am here to report, to balance on the gunwale of a canoe while wearing shin guards and attempting to synchronize your acrobatics with those of another paddler who is likewise balancing on a gunwale. Scooting on ice was hard; scooting through water or slush harder still. Around my foot and shin there formed a glassy shell of ice. It felt as if someone had lashed a dumbbell to my ankle.

"Let's go play in the ice!" Robitaille said. Attempting to transition, I leapt to the gunwales prematurely. The canoe rocked hard to starboard under my weight, almost chucking one of my teammates overboard. A bucketful or two of slush sloshed into the hull. I tumbled to port, righting the canoe but also landing hard on my seat, derailing it.

We kept going a little while longer, but the flood tide was accelerating, and we found ourselves caught on the treadmill, going nowhere. Before turning back and heading for shore, Robitaille gave us a short break.

We rested our oars, let the tide carry us, and as my heart began to decelerate, I was overcome by euphoria. I saw that it was magnificent out there, spinning around on the circling currents.

On the pier beside Bassin Louise, the snow had finally stopped. The tide and river had attained an eerie equilibrium. This happens a few times every day. The ice goes still, the floes lying atop their own reflections. It is, in these moments, as if the river is holding its breath.

The frenzied ice canoes, grinding into and out of the frozen basin, broke the spell—so many of them, it was hard to tell which were coming and which were going.

Out on the river, canoe number 181 and the blue canoe of Team Volvo had both turned onto the last leg of the third lap, the race's final stretch. Team Frontenac had opened up a small lead. Again, Lessard and Gilbert faced the choice: crowded channel or detour through the ice. Again Lessard chose the ice, and this time Gilbert followed, but not directly in Lessard's path, and the course Gilbert charted was the better one. Scooting, Team Volvo gained, pulling up portside to canoe 181, and then, fighting for the best lane, with a great clattering of oars, the two canoes collided. Out of the collision Volvo pulled ahead.

Meanwhile, neither Lessard nor Gilbert nor any of their teammates had noticed canoe 492, sponsored by La Capitale Groupe Financier. They hadn't noticed canoe 492 because no one on Team Volvo or Team Château Frontenac considered Team La Capitale a threat. In the first race of the season, at Portneuf, they'd placed seventh out of ten. In the second, at Rimouski, they hadn't bothered to compete. Now, while Volvo and Château Frontenac were battling it out, La Capitale's barreur navigated up the crowded channel skillfully, or perhaps luckily, avoiding collisions. His team slipped into Bassin Louise in first place. "*Mon dieu!*" the sportscaster shouted. "Not Château Frontenac! Not Volvo! It's the big surprise of the day! Canoe number 492! La Capitale! Wow!"

This is how an ice-canoe race ends: with a final charge across the frozen basin to the finish line. Canoe 492 scooted beneath the pneumatic arch unchallenged. The ruts in the ice were so deep now, they'd become like canals, which made passing difficult. In front of canoe 181, blocking the way, Volvo seemed to have a lock on second place, but, entering the basin, they made an unforced error. Instead of scooting toward the pneumatic finish line, they scooted in the direction of the target to the left of it. "We were a bit excited about all that was happening—the missing oar, Frontenac just beside us, finishing the race," Gilbert later told me. "We lost focus for a moment."

Jean Anderson saw his opening, and his team accelerated into a kind of one-legged sprint. Team Volvo had noticed their error and were trying to correct it, steering to the right, aiming for the finish line, but now it was a matter of geometry. The angle of Anderson's path was smaller than the angle available to Team Volvo, and canoe 181 passed under the arch first, in second place, Volvo's blue canoe following moments after.

In Michel Lessard's minivan, we rode through the narrow, slushy streets of Canada's oldest city, ascending the bluff in silence. Lessard was convinced they'd raced the wrong canoe. Number 79 would have performed better in the snow, he told me. In 2016, when they'd won the Super Bowl of *canot à glace*, a press conference had accompanied the celebration in the banquet hall of Château Frontenac. There were no members of the press in attendance this year, only me. At the hotel's entrance, Lessard handed his minivan's keys to the valet and climbed the marble steps. He'd taken off his crampons but was otherwise still outfitted for a sprint on the river.

Château Frontenac was never an actual château. Some of the buildings on the nearby streets date from the 1600s. The hotel itself was built in 1892. It is a Gilded Age ostentation, dressed up with conical towers to resemble a medieval castle. In the hotel's banquet hall, waiters in black aprons and white shirts had put out a buffet of dishes under silver lids. Amid an array of fruits and cheeses, an enormous ice sculpture, depicting a boatload of canotiers, had begun to melt.

All of the round banquet tables were empty but one around which the members of Team Château Frontenac had gathered to commiserate. However dispiriting, their defeat was temporary. The following week in Montreal, I'd watch them win easily, passing under the arch three and a half minutes ahead of Volvo. They'd place second in the last three races of the season—Sorel-Tracy, Isle-aux-Coudres, and Grand Défi—and in these last two races, it would be Team Volvo that would best them; but having placed in every race, with three wins for the season to Volvo's two, Château Frontenac would be crowned the 2017 champions of the ice-canoe circuit once again.

In the banquet hall, I took a seat beside Eric Fraser. He'd had to give up ice canoeing two years before on account of a new job designing snowshoes for a sporting-goods company. The job required him to make frequent trips to factories in China. He missed racing and still sometimes went out with the team on training runs for the fun of it. On a big screen here in the banquet hall, he and other spectators had watched a live feed of the race.

When I'd asked other canotiers what had drawn them to the sport, many spoke nostalgically about the connection to local history, some about needing to be outdoors during Quebec's depressingly long winter. Most spoke about their love of the Saint Lawrence. When I put the question to Fraser, who speaks fluent English, he told me about the nocturnal training

runs. Since the training schedule in ice canoeing is determined
by the tides, and since winter days are short, the members of
Anderson's team often have no choice but to go out on the river
before sunrise or after dark. "It's superb. It's poetic. It's majes-
tic," Fraser said. "We'll stop the boat. Five grown men. Not
talking. Just looking." He searched for the words to explain it.
"Because the movement is so fluid, you don't feel movement.
You feel the environment is moving for you."

The day after the big race, I drive north. I want to follow the
Saint Lawrence to its mouth. Way up at Godbout, where the
river ends and the Gulf begins, there's a car ferry that crosses to
the far shore. I've booked a ticket. In winter, the ferry departs
just once a day, at 5 P.M. sharp, and I'm running late. North of
Quebec City, the highway veers away from the river and up into
the mountains of the Canadian Shield. My phone dies. The
charger won't work. I stop at a gas station to squeegee my windshield and purchase a map, then speed on. The road plunges
out of the mountains to the edge of the Saguenay River where
it empties into the Saint Lawrence. There's no bridge. You have
to cross on an open-decked ferry. On the Saguenay's north
bank, the highway resumes. There's a village there, Tadoussac.
I pull off to see it. Tadoussac is among the oldest settlements in
North America. Half a millennium ago, it was here that colonists from France often first set foot on North American soil.
Prior to the arrival of the French, the Innu had a hunting camp
and trading post here. On September 1, 1535, on his second voyage, explorer Jacques Cartier landed at Tadoussac and found
"four boats" (canoes) in which "Canadians" (a band of local
Innu) were "fishing for sea-wolves" (hunting seals). North of

Tadoussac, the highway keeps roller-coasting along, following the mountainous shore of the Saint Lawrence, sheer granite cliffs dropping off to the river below.

We don't think of the Great Lakes as a river, but that's what they are: immense, deep interruptions in a slow-moving stream 2,300 miles long—as long, approximately, as the Mississippi— and the last 743 miles of that stream we call the Saint Lawrence. Water in western Lake Superior will eventually, after 300 years, make its way here. At the river's end, I'm not sure what I hope to find. Maybe I'm wishing that highways, like the Saint Lawrence, could rewind.

Canoes, Sieur de Lahontan noted in 1683, are the "voitures" of North America. In his era, voitures were horse-drawn carriages. In ours, voitures are cars. It's true: In the seventeenth century, canoes were, in the interior of the continent, North America's preferred utility vehicle. "In these slender contrivances," Lahontan wrote, "the Canadians perform all their Voyages." People didn't climb into them seeking a wilderness experience, or an athletic challenge, or an endorphin rush, an intensification of time. They climbed into them for the same reason that, this morning, in a hurry, I'd climbed behind the wheel of my station wagon: to get where they needed to go with what they needed to carry as safely and as swiftly as possible. Maybe centuries from now—it occurs to me, as I speed north to Godbout—people will race station wagons on some ruined remnant of interstate.

I make it to Godbout by a quarter to five, just in time. The sun is already setting. The cars queued up for the ferry are numerous. It takes a while for us to board. By the time we embark, night has fallen. There's no moon. With my face pressed to a window, I look out over the bow into the darkness. In the ferry's running lights, ghostly floes appear and vanish. We are crossing the mouth of the Saint Lawrence. I give up trying to see out into the darkness. I listen instead to the noisy music of the steel hull, which plays alternately rumbling and silent variations on the water and ice as we travel along the imaginary line between the river and the sea.

WATERMARKS

> Where does a story begin? The fiction is that they do, and
> end, rather than that the stuff of a story is just a cup of
> water scooped from the sea and poured back into it.
>
> —*Rebecca Solnit*

> In an age when man has forgotten his origins and is
> blind even to his most essential needs for survival, water
> along with other resources has become the victim of
> his indifference.
>
> —*Rachel Carson*

In 1849, after hearing Emerson deliver the lecture "Mind &
Manners in the Nineteenth Century," Melville, in one of
his bouts of enthusiasm, scribbled a letter to a friend. "I love
all men who *dive*," he declared. The first time I read that dec-
laration, I pictured Ralph Waldo at the end of a diving board
wearing a swimsuit—a full-body swimsuit, perhaps, of the sort
that might have been fashionable at the time—and maybe an
oilskin swimmer's cap, a pair of goggles made of, I don't know,
isinglass. This is pure fancy, of course. The high dive had not
been invented in 1849. Nor had Americans yet learned to chlo-
rinate water or domesticate the swimming pool. Water in 1849
was for ablutions and baptisms; for drinking; for irrigating

fields and powering mills; for harvesting in its various phases—vapor, liquid, ice; for traveling over in boats. Keep reading Melville's letter and it becomes clear that he's picturing a different sort of diver. He's imagining Emerson as a kind of philosophical whale, sounding the depths.

At the time he wrote that letter, wagon trains were leaving Missouri, heading west. A year later, in 1850, when Melville began work on *Moby-Dick*, he included in its opening chapter a meditation on the metaphysics of water with some dubious advice for the Pioneers: "Let the most absent-minded of men be plunged in his deepest reveries—stand that man on his legs, set his feet a-going, and he will infallibly lead you to water, if water there be in all that region." Perhaps thinking of Emerson, he adds: "Should you ever be athirst in the great American desert, try this experiment, if your caravan happen to be supplied with a metaphysical professor. Yes, as every one knows meditation and water are wedded for ever."

~

And if your company does not include a metaphysical professor? If you found yourself without water, out there in the great American desert in 1849? Or in the parched precincts of Cape Town in 2018? What then?

Accounts come down to us, among them a vivid report filed in 1906 by an adventuresome scientist named W. J. McGee, who investigates the thirsty case of a wayward prospector named Pablo Valencia. Valencia had barely survived for "nearly seven days" without water in the summer heat of the Arizona Territory, snacking on scorpions and drinking his own urine. Having examined the patient's symptoms, McGee divides the physiol-

ogy of thirst into three stages. There is "the stage of normal dry-
ness," familiar to all of us. Then comes "the stage of functional
derangement." The tongue clings to the teeth. The eustachian
tubes burn. The skin tightens painfully over the skull like the
head of a drum. The brain and spine ache. The voice cracks.
The mind begins to go: "unreasoned revulsions arise against
persons and things, while water and wetness are subcon-
sciously exalted as the end of all excellence." Finally comes "the
stage of structural degeneration," which is as bad as it sounds,
characterized by McGee as "a progressive mummification of
the initially living body."

Life as we know it can survive without sunlight or oxygen:
Witness the creatures that populate the sulfurous vicinity of
submarine geothermal vents. Life as we know it cannot live
without water, and where there is water, there is almost always
life. "I discovered living creatures in rain, which had stood but
a few days in a new tub," Antonie van Leeuwenhoek observed
in 1675 after peering through his invention, a new and better
microscope. A grown man like Pablo Valencia can last three
weeks without food; without water, at most several days. For
good reason, in its search for extraterrestrial life, NASA has
defined the "habitable zone" as "the distance from a star where
one can have liquid water on the surface of a planet." We earth-
lings are at no risk of exiting our sun's habitable zone anytime
soon, but the reports arriving from McGee's successors—of
rising waters in Miami and Bangladesh, of poisoned waters in
Fiji and Flint, of dwindling reservoirs and depleted aquifers—
are troubling enough to make one wonder if the entire planet
has already entered a stage of derangement. Clean water in
this coming century, credible oracles predict, will become

more valuable than oil, an accelerant to conflagration as well as conflagration's antidote. The aging waterworks of America, meanwhile, seem well on their way toward McGee's stage of structural degeneration.

Explore the history of water-writing and you'll find that literary hydrography is slippery, shape-shifting, ever-changing, difficult to chart, turbulent one moment and the next stilled by a glassy calm, and sometimes beneath a calm you can detect a hidden turbulence, like the invisible resonances of a seiche. This much, I'm prepared to hazard: Literary hydrography is almost always thirsty, almost always an exaltation of water and wetness.

Writers walk the banks of rivers, from the Danube to the Yangtze to the Nile. They embark. They put on waders and get out their sampling jars. They dowse. They sound. They visit aqueducts and public baths and bottling plants. They dive—sometimes without leaving their desks. Like the cub river pilot Samuel Clemens, they read ripples, fathom depths, follow currents, decipher water's secrets. They seek to acquire fluency in fluency. "I am haunted by waters," Norman Maclean wrote from the banks of the Blackfoot River. "I am haunted by waters," Olivia Laing repeats, in affirmation, from the banks of the River Ouse.

~

Growing up in San Francisco's semisuburban outskirts during the drought years of the 1970s, I learned early on to treat water not only as an elemental source—of life and cleanliness, meditation and metaphor—but as that drier abstraction, a natural resource. The California of my childhood was the one Joan

Didion wrote about the year I turned five, the coastal terminus of the American West, a region whose borders were drawn by drought. "The West begins where the average annual rainfall drops below twenty inches," Bernard DeVoto wrote, a definition Didion endorses, and to which she attributes her own "reverence for water"—for water and in her case for the waterworks with which Westerners had made deserts bring forth orange groves and swimming pools. Where Didion saw order wrung from nature's chaos, adoptive Westerner Edward Abbey saw order's illusion, evidence of hubris and folly. Didion would venerate a dam that Abbey would blow up. Water invites such contradictions. It purifies and corrupts, sustains life and destroys it. Water rusts and rots, and it preserves. "Kinds of water drown us. Kinds of water do not," Anne Carson writes, distilling the conundrum to a riddle.

Our family dutifully obeyed the exhortations issued by local officials: Let the lawn yellow, the station wagon gather dust. Turn the faucet off while brushing your teeth. These austere rituals required a suspension of disbelief and a faith in the wisdom of bureaucrats, for the world as we experienced it appeared in no danger of running short of water. If you left the faucet on, the water ran until you shut the faucet off, and when wildfires broke out in the golden hills, as they did almost every summer, the fire trucks never failed to answer the alarm, and with rare exception, the hydrants summoned forth from beneath the sidewalk a gusher commensurate with the flames.

My parents were both churchgoers, and when I first encountered the opening chapters of the Bible, I recognized the description there of an earthly realm stretched between waters above and waters below. Our house occupied a foggy altitude, and its windows often opened onto heavens of mist—evaporate from the Pacific that would condense in the cooling air, rolling in and out like a tide. When the fog washed onto the mountains of California's coastal range, it turned their upper slopes into a littoral zone, their peaks into islands, our cul-de-sac of stucco row houses—painted the pastels of a coral reef—into a foggy Atlantis.

Collecting in the branches of the redwoods and eucalyptus trees, the fog watered the ferny understory of the temperate forests. On those rare occasions when a downpour broke the dry spell, the slopes would liquefy. The evening news would feature footage of highways and bungalows buried under mud. A culvert beside our neighbor's house channeled rivulets of runoff to the curbside gutter where it swelled into a little river, my own diminutive Mississippi on whose muddy waters I would perform experiments in hydrology, building dams of pebbles and dirt, studying currents, setting leaves adrift—efforts at water management that were as futile as those of the Army Corps of Engineers during the Great Flood of 1927, as futile in the long run as most human efforts to control water and contain it. The curbside rivulet always found its way to the sewer grate by the lamppost, where it would disappear into a mysterious darkness out of which there rose an odor of swamp. Anyone requiring a lesson in the hazards of flood control need only read John McPhee's account of his travels around the Louisiana Delta or Jesmyn Ward's *Salvage the Bones,* a novel set in the mayhem of Hurricane Katrina, or revisit the footage aired in the autumn of 2018 when the waters above and below conspired to inundate Houston and San Juan. Water is the universal solvent, of schemes as well as substances.

In motion, it seems alive, motivated by a kind purpose as it seeks its level, its surface sinuous, muscular, as if animated by serpents or spirits, which helps explain all those fantastic monsters and mermaids and river gods that have populated the waters of the human mind. All matter is in motion, physicists and Heraclitus tell us, but the motion of water, unlike that of atoms or stone, readily accommodates our powers of perception, the time scale of a human life. The motion of water is luminous and momentary. No wonder so many writers throughout the centuries, while walking beside a river or a Venetian canal, have like Joseph Brodsky glimpsed through their own reflections a metaphor for time. Da Vinci, in his notebooks, made plans for a treatise on water in which he would "describe all the shapes that water assumes from its greatest to its smallest wave." I understand the impulse.

~

Lapsed though I am, I'm still stirred by the poetics of the flood in Genesis 6—how the fountains of the deep burst forth and the windows of heaven open. Judaism, Christianity, Islam—they may all be "desert religions," sure, but they are also, like most faiths people have observed all over the world and throughout the recorded centuries, religions of water. The Bible is a soggy book. Witness how many miracles and divine interventions occur on water, or at its edge. In 2 Kings a leper named Naaman takes a curative dip in the spa of the Jordan River. John the Baptist spends his days there, busy as the attendant of a profitable car wash. Jonah, that reluctant aquanaut, quiets the Mediterranean. Moses bloodies the Nile, parts the Red Sea, and in his downtime meets his future wife at a watering hole.

Jesus saunters around, barefoot as a water skeeter, on the surface of Galilee. For good reason many religious pilgrimages terminate in sources and springs. The Quran is likewise soggy, promising faithful believers an afterlife with "gardens graced with flowing streams" and "rivers of water forever pure." Every living thing in the Quran is made of water. "To a desert culture," writes historian Garry Wills, "water is not only needed for life. It is life. It is the material thing nearest to God." In a desert, all waters are holy.

Then again, people sanctify water in rainy latitudes too. In Vietnamese, the word for water is also the word for homeland. And in polar ones. Several summers ago, I found myself taking a walk under the midnight sun along the shores of the Northwest Passage accompanied by an Inuit kid named Puglik. In the mining town of Cambridge Bay, where we'd met, many working adults sleep through the sunlit night. Their children, some of them, play by night and sleep by day. I was staying with an archaeologist who'd spent the summer field season, now nearly over, excavating a Thule house pit on the town's outskirts. As the Arctic permafrost thaws, such sites, preserved for centuries, are at risk of melting away, and my archaeologist friend thought I might like to see one while I had the chance. On our way out of town we ran into Puglik kicking at the bark chips under the monkey bars of a public playground. He was underdressed in what looked like hand-me-downs: a navy hooded sweatshirt with sleeves long enough to warm his fingertips and a pair of white sneakers so big I could have worn them. Bored, he asked to join us.

The road was muddy. The Arctic in summer's thaw is a muddy place, muddier and muddier as the planet warms. For underdressed pilgrims on a hike, however, the weather was still plenty cold. A wind refrigerated by sea ice was giving us all the shivers, and Puglik kept wiping his nose with his sleeve, carrying on about his favorite video games and pointing out local landmarks. In a graveyard atop a hill, wooden crosses had begun to topple and tilt. His ancestors were all buried there, at least the ones he knew about, Puglik said, but now the entire hill was thawing, the graveyard slowly sliding toward the sea.

To windward flowed a glassy stream in which you could see a weir, a funnel of rocks with which locals corralled fish for easy harvesting, as people had been doing since the ice sheets retreated. The stream was popular with migrating waterfowl as well as fish. Geese that had wintered in Biloxi nested here on the tundra. We know that migrating birds follow spring. They're chasing sunlight, of course, but they're also chasing wetlands; they too make pilgrimages to water. We came to a bend in the road that conformed to a bend in the stream, and in the stream's bend was an eddy that conformed to some invisible bend in the cosmos, deep enough for a swimming hole. "We call this part of the river," Puglik said, "'an Inuit Jacuzzi.'"

I'd come to Cambridge Bay in the company of scientists studying its changing ecology and climate, and while traveling through the Northwest Passage aboard an icebreaker, I'd joined a cryologist with the Canadian Ice Service on a survey conducted by helicopter. The cryologist—or "Ice Pick" as people in her line of work are colloquially known—had to chart and classify the puzzling ice pack visible below. Although it had thawed and thinned earlier than it had in any year on record, there remained a multitude of ice to see and classify. The names for its varieties, I learned, are as numerous and lovely as those for clouds: *frazil, pancake, nilas, grease, agglomerated brash.* The language of ice describes more than dimensions and shapes. It names subtle gradations in the phase changes water undergoes as it solidifies and expands or liquefies and condenses.

With our terrestrial eyes, we are good at perceiving and classifying water in its solid and vaporous forms. The vernacular for liquid water is meager by comparison. Since the time of the ancient Phoenicians, if not before, navigators and river pilots have learned to read water's surface well, but it is only over the past century or so that limnologists and oceanographers have begun studying and classifying underwater formations shaped by chemistry and thermodynamics—dense masses drifting through the twilight zone like underwater clouds, or vortices spinning around like underwater storms. We're still acquiring fluency in fluency.

~

These days I live in southeast Michigan, which is to say I dwell in a watershed of paradox. Here we are, at the edge of the Great Lakes, which together contain 84 percent of North America's and 20 percent of the world's accessible freshwater. The Great Lakes are puddles of glacial melt. Rainfall and tributaries contribute only 1 percent of their total volume. Much of the rest is "fossil water," sequestered from the water cycle since the last ice age. Under a recently issued state permit, the Nestlé corporation, a major purveyor of bottled water, can now draw up to 400 gallons of Michigan groundwater per minute for just $200 a year. And yet in Flint people now regard their faucets with warranted suspicion, and in Detroit, whose water treatment plant would have spared the people of Flint from mass poisoning, the water company has been turning the spigots off, letting their delinquent customers go thirsty or purchase bottled water from Nestlé.

During the federal emergency in Flint, I spent some time in the city, following a team of civil engineers conducting an investigation. I watched as contractors excavated a residential street, extracting a service line from under the asphalt. The line—a few dozen yards of copper pipe—was evidence at a crime scene, and the scientists labeled it with forensic care. Looking at it coiled on a sun-dappled lawn, dirt still clinging to the copper, I experienced a feeling that I later recognized as disenchantment. What I couldn't get over was how small the pipe's diameter was: three-quarters of an inch. This was it? The source of the everyday magic?

For most of my life, running water had been one of those technologies, like the telephone or electric light, that I took for granted. Where the water came from and where it went when it gurgled down the drain were both mysteries that I'd only rarely wondered about. Living in the age of indoor plumbing is a bit like living beside a stream whose headwaters and mouth are distant rumors. The waterworks of wealthy nations, or at least those of certain zip codes, are a kind of manmade River Lethe. In Imperial Rome, the aqueduct was a public monument as well as an engineering feat. Buried underground, our own aqueducts invite forgetting. In New York, the subterranean water tunnels constitute, writes David Grann, "a city under the city," one that few New Yorkers know about, let alone ever see.

We forget the value and scarcity of potable water. Most of the planet's 332 million cubic miles of water is salty. "Only 2 percent is fresh," Rose George reports in her 2008 study of human waste, *The Big Necessity*, "and two thirds of that is unavailable for human use, locked in snow, ice, and permafrost." We forget how much of it we waste—we Americans, especially. While about a billion people get by on five liters of water a day, Americans use more than twice that in a single toilet flush. We forget the people—some 30 percent of the global population—who do not have easy access to safe drinking water. We forget what life was like prior to the advent of chlorination.

For reminders, we can read the diary that Carolina Maria de Jesus kept in 1958, documenting the daily life of a São Paulo favela whose inhabitants lined up every morning at a public spigot and fished from a polluted lagoon. We can visit Victorian London and witness cholera spread from a single contaminated pump, or make a pilgrimage to the sacred grotto of Lourdes, where in 1894 Zola watched the Catholic faithful immerse themselves in "a frightful *consommé* of all ailments, a field of cultivation for every kind of poisonous germ, a quintessence of the most dreaded contagious disease."

During one of my trips to Flint, I went to have a look at the city's notorious river. The downtown promenade was buried deep in snow. A single pedestrian had gone promenading anyway, leaving behind a trail of boot prints that led from the salted sidewalks of Saginaw Street down a flight of concrete stairs to the concrete quay at the river's edge. I followed them. A hundred yards upstream, the Flint frothed and boiled through an open lock, but by the time it reached me, its surface had settled to a low simmer. To the naked eye, it didn't look so bad. I wasn't tempted to kneel down and fill up a canteen—the water was opaque and khaki green, like rancid olive oil—but dead fish weren't floating on its surface. If I'd dropped a match, it wouldn't have caught fire, as the Cuyahoga and the Chicago used to. The air above it didn't stink. Having once gone boating on the Des Plaines River, outflow of Chicago's Sanitary and Ship Canal, and having visited the Hudson after a rainstorm had overwhelmed Manhattan's storm drains, I'd seen and smelled worse. Upstream from me, a pair of Canada geese on a snowy bank appeared to be enjoying their waterfront view. If I hadn't known better, I'd never have guessed that I was looking at the wellsprings of disaster.

This is yet another source of water's mystery: Its exact makeup is inscrutable to the naked eye, and to our other senses. You need a compound microscope or a mass spectrometer to determine whether you've filled your drinking glass with the waters of life or a *consommé* of ailments. What discolored the sampling bottles Flint's residents had held before the television cameras in 2015 was iron corroded from rusty pipes. Corroded lead, once dissolved, is odorless and invisible.

～

Whenever I visit a river, I have the urge to follow it. The Flint flows west, and if I'd continued my promenade in that direction, I'd have reached, fifty miles downstream, the confluence with the Shiawassee, which flows northeast into the Saginaw, which empties into Saginaw Bay, which opens onto Lake Huron, which is itself in truth an immense caesura in a slow-moving stream whose headwaters lie at the western end of Lake Superior and whose terminus is the Gulf of Saint Lawrence, which opens onto the North Atlantic. The journey of a river from source to mouth resembles our own journey from birth to death, an analogy oft remarked, and yet the beginnings and endings of rivers are as fictional as those we impose on stories. There are headwaters to headwaters and no river ever really ends.

I have over several years followed the water through the outskirts of Chicago, over Niagara Falls, down the Mississippi. I've traveled Lake Erie by sailboat, the Saint Lawrence by canoe, chasing a ghost geography, a relic map, hidden behind the pixelated roads and interstates charted by my Global Positioning System. Since moving to Michigan, trying to understand the place, I've studied its recorded history, which does have a beginning, in the accounts written in the seventeenth century by the French. Flipping in chronological order through their hand-drawn maps, you can watch the familiar geography emerge as if out of the water. At first, water is all there is, a meandering of riverbanks and coastlines in the midst of a vast blankness. Even the place names are watery. "Michigan" is transliterated Algonquian for "Big Water," and all around the Great Lakes are towns and streets named for rapids and portages. The early history of the American Midwest was written from the vantage of a canoe. "Rivers must have been the guides which conducted the footsteps of the first travellers," wrote Thoreau after voyaging with his brother on the Concord and the Merrimack. "They are the constant lure, when they flow by our doors, to distant enterprise and adventure; and, by a natural impulse, the dwellers on their banks will at length accompany their currents to the lowlands of the globe, or explore at their invitation the interior of continents."

In the twenty-first century, it's not easy to follow the water. Beyond downtown riverfront promenades, one enters a semi-feral, semi-industrial no-man's-land, an inside-out version of

America hidden from the view from a sidewalk or a driver's seat. Along the Lower Mississippi, between the levees and the water's edge, the river's flood stages have kept development at bay, preserving an accidental wetland wilderness, a landscape of incongruities accessible only by boat. Haul out beside the outflows of petrochemical refineries, climb over the batture and through the willows, watching for fire ant mounds and poison ivy, and you can emerge onto the shores of a nameless pond, the remnant of an oxbow meander where alligators are sunning in the shallows and a hundred roseate spoonbills and pelicans, startled by your startlement, burst loudly into flight.

~

Below the water's surface lie more lost worlds. Water remembers what we might otherwise forget, in part because what we wish to forget, we jettison. We pretend that to throw something into the East River or the ocean is to make it disappear, when really its disappearance is an illusion, a vanishing act. The Great Lakes, I've learned, are especially good at remembering. In the cold, fresh, oxygen-depleted refrigerator of their depths, wrecks and other sunken relics last longer than they would in the ocean, where salt corrodes metal, and wood becomes food for teredo worms. In Thunder Bay, at the northwestern edge of Lake Huron, there is a kind of underwater museum—the Thunder Bay National Marine Sanctuary, it's called. Visit the sanctuary's website and you can go diving without leaving your desk. Shipwrecks appear on a map. Click on one, and the name of some doomed vessel pops up, alongside spooky photographs of its phantasmal remains.

Here is the steel freighter *Norman,* which during the Gilded Age ferried ore to the Globe Iron Works in Cleveland, Ohio, and now sits in two hundred feet of water, where it has grown popular with zebra mussels. Here is the *Montana,* which caught fire in 1914. Here is the delightfully named *Typo,* a three-masted schooner erased from the lake surface by a fast-moving steamer in 1899. Four sailors drowned. The *Typo* is still carrying a load of coal it will never deliver, and a ship's bell still hangs in the belfry. If you were willing to piss off the archaeological custodians in charge of Thunder Bay and risk tangling your flippers in the ancient riggings, you could swim down to the decks of the *Typo* and give the bell a ring. Had any of these vessels made it to safe harbor, they would likely be long gone.

There's a bumper sticker popular in these parts that shows a map of the five Great Lakes beside the caption UNSALTED, SHARK-FREE. The first time I saw it, it occurred to me that an opportunity had presented itself. Suffering from a phobia of sharks, I'd never gone scuba diving, though I'd wanted to. And so, not long ago, after completing the requisite training, I found myself perched on the rail of a fishing boat, tugging a pair of flippers on over a pair of neoprene booties.

The fishing boat was anchored off Poverty Island, one of several in a chain of uninhabited islands at the northern end of Lake Michigan that obstruct the entrance to Green Bay. Also aboard the fishing boat was a shipwreck hunter and a team of commercial divers he'd hired. The shipwreck hunter had spent three decades and upward of a million dollars searching for a wooden French brigantine last seen in 1679. He was convinced he was on the verge of finding it. The trail of clues he'd assembled in the historical archives seemed to him unassailable, and he'd brought me along to document his triumph. Not all men who dive are philosophers, I now know. Some of them are retirees squandering their life fortunes on misbegotten hunts for missing ships.

In emails, the shipwreck hunter had referred to our outing as an expedition and had dressed accordingly, which is to say nautically, in a navy-blue windbreaker and a navy ball cap embroidered with golden laurels. On the windbreaker, stitched over his heart, was a date, 1679, and the name of the ship, *Le Griffon*, for which he had spent most of his adulthood searching. A little icon of the ship sailed above his ball cap's bill encircled by the words IMAGINE, EXPLORE, DISCOVER. He'd meant to bring matching *Le Griffon* T-shirts for everyone aboard the fishing boat to make the expedition feel more expeditionary, but he'd forgotten them back at his condo. This trivial oversight seemed to fill him with outsized regret.

Connected to the surface by a braid of hoses known, poetically, as "the umbilical," the commercial divers had gone overboard one by one, wearing "hard hats," modern-day versions of the diving helmets worn by the aquanauts you might encounter in an illustrated edition of Jules Verne, or seated on a plastic treasure chest at the bottom of a decorative aquarium. Walking around in weighted boots, scanning the lakebed with handheld magnetometers, the commercial divers hadn't found much aside from driftwood. The Great Lakes are good at remembering; they're also good at obliterating. Nevertheless, the shipwreck hunter had agreed to send me down, and the time had come.

Perched on the rail of the fishing boat, tugging on my flippers, wearing a rented seven-millimeter wet suit, I was beset by second thoughts. At scuba school the instructor had elaborated in memorable detail the assorted gruesome ways that scuba diving can abbreviate a life, the most memorable of which to my mind was this: Ascend too quickly without exhaling, and your lungs will pop like balloons. At bottom, sixty feet down, it would be a comparatively warm 38 degrees Fahrenheit. Sometimes, at the bottom of the Great Lakes, under the hazy pane of the thermocline, liquid water descends below 32 degrees without freezing, on account of the pressure. Into their suits, the commercial divers had pumped, through one of the hoses braided into the umbilical, heated water. The shipwreck hunter had told me that my exposed face might feel as if it had been "stung by bees," but a seven-millimeter suit would be warm enough, he'd assured me.

In my head, to calm myself, I recited the opening lines of Adrienne Rich's "Diving into the Wreck":

> First having read the book of myths,
> and loaded the camera,
> and checked the edge of the knife-blade,
> I put on
> the body-armor of black rubber
> the absurd flippers
> the grave and awkward mask.

You may think this an embellishment, that perched on the rail of a fishing boat, squeezing your nostrils shut, preparing to tumble backward overboard, you'd have better things to think about than a poem, but I promise you I'd committed those lines to memory—because I wanted to write about the experience someday, yes, but also because I wanted more than the bright white nylon anchor line to guide me down into Lake Michigan's cerulean immensity, and because I wanted to remember why it was I was doing this. I was doing this because I'd imagined that descending the water column would be like time travel, like flippering into the past, as if fathoms were centuries.

MIDWEST PASSAGE

The first edition of the map had to be colored by hand. The surviving copies therefore differ. On the copy held by the National Archives, the water is a washed-out turquoise, the parchment showing through. On the copy belonging to the Archives Nationales de Québec, the water's a shade closer to robin's egg, and the North American continent—painted a tawny yellow, speckled with little black trees—resembles a badly damaged cheetah pelt. Across the top of every surviving copy, above the Arctic's *Mer Glaciale* there floats a banner along which runs a legend that in translation reads "New Discoveries of Many Nations in New France in the years 1673 and 1674." This legend, I've learned, is a bit misleading.

Although the map's terrestrial features seem to have been drawn by a precocious if geographically confused child, its aquatic features are strikingly recognizable, and strikingly out of scale. It's as if we're peering down at North America through a magnifying glass poised over the Great Lakes. Get an actual magnifying glass, or click on a little positively charged icon of one hovering over a hi-res jpeg, zoom in until the semilegible words inscribed along the coasts and riverbanks come into focus, and you'll recognize some familiar place names. "Illinois" is there. So's "Detroit." You'll also see names that sound

like something out of *Gulliver's Travels*. What we call Green
Bay is here labeled *Baye des Puans*, the Bay of Stinkards. Away
from the water's edge, the local place names disappear. This
isn't really a map of North America, certainly not as we now
know it, nor even of seventeenth-century New France and the
many nations newly discovered there; it's a navigation chart,
and a relic of a time when waterways assumed out-of-scale proportions in our geographies.

The map was drawn from memory by the explorer Louis
Joliet, whose otherwise successful 1673–1674 expedition to
the Mississippi ended disastrously, in the rapids of the Saint
Lawrence River just south of Montreal—a capsized canoe, two
voyageurs and an Ojibwe guide drowned, Joliet clinging to the
rocks, a cargo of precious documents (including his maps) lost
to the currents and to history. Somehow he made it to shore,
dried off, and by August 1, 1674, had found his way to the Jesuit
Mission in Quebec. In a debriefing conducted by Father Superior Claude Daublon, the weary explorer did his best to salvage
from the currents of his mind everything of the expedition he
could remember—or at least everything of geopolitical and
mercantile importance to the Jesuit mission and the French
Empire; Joliet's personal memories of his travels, his impres-
sions of the American interior and of the people who lived
there, are as irretrievable as the documents lost to the rapids.

On their expedition, Joliet and his priestly traveling compan-
ion Père Marquette had descended the Mississippi as far as its
confluence with the Arkansas, where, having determined that
the river flowed south not west, they turned back. They hadn't
found the passage to the Pacific they'd hoped to find, but what
they had found was almost as good: a trade route through the

heart of the continent by which—Joliet reported to Daublon—
"a bark" could sail "with great facility" and "by very easy navigation" from "New France" to "Florida," or as we would put it,
from Canada to the Gulf Coast. It is this discovery, this route,
that Joliet's hand-drawn navigation chart illustrates.

For the French, ice-bound along the St. Lawrence River, a
navigable waterway to the Gulf promised access to a warm-
water port, and by laying claim to it and the territory around
it, they could hem in their imperial rivals—the English and
Dutch to the East, the Spaniards to the south. There was just
one obstacle to overcome, identified on his map by the word
"portage," written at the site of present-day Chicago. There, at
the southwestern tip of Lake Michigan, the explorers had been
obliged to lug their cargo and canoes across the "half a league
of prairie" separating a tributary of the Mississippi, now known
as the Des Plaines, from the Chicago River, which in 1673 still
flowed east into the nearby lake.

Today, drivers on I-55 speed over that half a league of prairie, thinking nothing of it. Commuters on the Forest Park
Branch of the Blue Line of the "L" cross most of that prairie if
they stay on to the last stop. Across Harlem Avenue from British Petroleum's Chicago oil terminal, a National Historic Site
has preserved one sad, soggy remnant of the old portage, and
commemorated it with an Art Nouveau sculpture of rusty steel
that depicts a grim-faced Père Marquette pointing east toward
Lake Michigan while Joliet and an anonymous *voyageur* in
fringed buckskin do the hard labor of canoe portaging. So far
as canoe portages went, half a league wasn't much—around
1.5 miles—but you couldn't sail across a prairie in a bark, with
or without great facility.

Joliet, however, had an idea, one that would eventually alter the history of the continent, as well as its ecology: "It would only be necessary," the explorer suggests and Daublon records, "to make a canal."

Although Joliet didn't know it, what he and Marquette had discovered at the southern tip of Lake Michigan, geologically speaking, was a low point on the subcontinental divide that cleaves the two great river basins of North America, the Mississippi Basin, which stretches from the Alleghenies to the foothills of the Rockies, and the Great Lakes Basin, which empties via the St. Lawrence into the Labrador Sea. Near the end of the last ice age, glacial melt from Lake Michigan had for a while drained south through the Chicago River, erasing the divide, flowing down the Des Plaines, into the Illinois, which joins the Mississippi fifty miles north of St. Louis. For a few prehistorical centuries, the waterway of Joliet's dreams had existed.

Around nine thousand years ago, as the ice sheet retreated, it piled up—right there at Joliet's portage, right there at BP's oil terminal—moraines of glacial till. Relieved of the weight of ice, a limestone ridge beneath the till rose up—a process known as glacial rebound or isostatic uplift. The rise was so slight, just several feet, that without a surveyor's transom, you might not have noticed it; so slight that in seasons of flood the rivers sometimes submerged it. But it was enough to subdivide the continent and disconnect the two great drainage basins—except during seasons of flood—for the next 10,000 years. Joliet, although he didn't know it, was proposing to reconnect them.

The task would prove more daunting than he realized, or maybe he realized how daunting it would prove but didn't let on, eager as he and other explorers were to secure the financial and political backing of church and crown. During the dry season, that "half a league of prairie" at the Chicago portage could grow to ten miles or more. The shortest path across it cut through Mud Lake, which one historian describes as "a large, leech-infested puddle," so shallow that in some seasons fur traders in heavily laden canoes, following Joliet's route, had to get out and push, wading their way across, stripping down to remove leeches when they reached the far side.

However far-fetched it may have been, once entered into the historical record, the navigable waterway Joliet imagined became a recurring dream. It exists today, but not for the reasons Joliet suggested it, not exactly. With the arrival of rail, the need for navigable trade routes was less pressing. What Chicago really needed was a sewer. Lacking one, it used the Chicago River, which emptied into Lake Michigan, the city's water supply. The Chicago Sanitary and Ship Canal (shovel day: September 3, 1892) would connect the Great Lakes to the Mississippi Valley, but it would also reverse the course of the Chicago River, flushing the city's sewage south. The idea when first proposed seemed a folly, a boondoggle in the making. Reverse a river! You might as well part the waters of Lake Michigan or turn back time. But in low-lying Chicago, the plan's proponents demonstrated, this miracle of engineering could in fact be performed: Dig a channel deep enough through the subcontinental divide, and gravity would do the rest.

The excavation lasted eight years and cost $33 million. On the eve of its completion, word came from St. Louis that attorneys were preparing to petition the Supreme Court, seeking an injunction to shut down the canal before it opened. The trustees of Chicago's sanitary district responded not with legal actions of their own but by overseeing the destruction by dynamite and steam-powered dredge of the sole remaining barrier holding back the waters of the Chicago River.

Two days later, the *Chicago Record* delivered good news: "Clear water in the Chicago River—water that was actually blue in color and had blocks of ice of a transparent green hue floating in it—caused people who crossed bridges over the Chicago River yesterday to stop and stare in amazement." The news from Missouri was gloomier: "Windy City Sewage Now Headed This Way" ran a headline in the *St. Louis Star*.

The Sanitary and Ship Canal was heralded as a triumph of that heroic age of American civil engineering in which technological progress and industrial might promised to deliver us from nature's tyranny. If we could reverse the course of rivers, what couldn't we bend to our will?

In 1955, the American Society of Civil Engineers named Chicago's sanitation system to its list of seven modern wonders. Also included: the Empire State Building and Hoover Dam. "Man, modern man—the scientist, the explorer, the builder of bridges and waterways and steam engines, the visionary entrepreneur—had become the central creative force," David McCullough wrote in *The Path Between the Seas,* his history of the Panama Canal (also on the list).

The view these days is muddier. Like many modern wonders, Chicago's canal solved the problem it was engineered to solve—the city's sewage crisis—but it did so by sending the consequences downstream, to the Mississippi Valley and, in unanticipated ways, to all of us. In hindsight, it looks less like a triumph of the heroic age of civil engineering than like a prologue to the chastening age we live in now, the epoch geologists have proposed calling the Anthropocene, the age of the sixth extinction. One cause of this extinction: the trade routes and flight paths and navigable waterways with which we stitched continents and basins together. Thanks to us, species that evolved in isolation now collide, at times with devastating effects on ecosystems.

A hundred or so years after it opened, Chicago's canal has been making news again. "Asian Carp DNA Found in Downtown Chicago, a Block from Lake Michigan" read a recent headline. You may have seen footage of the slapstick scenes in which boaters motor through a storm of airborne fish. The aerialists in those videos are all silver carp, the only of the four invasive species of Asian carp that exhibits the entertaining fright response so popular on YouTube. Another of the four, the bighead carp, is constitutionally furtive, difficult to catch or detect. By the time the Asian carp footage went viral on the Internet, both species had already gone viral in the Mississippi watershed. Voracious planktivores, they reproduce quickly. Fully grown, they have no natural predators except humans. Commercial fishermen on the Illinois River now catch 25,000 pounds of Asian carp per day, with little discernible effect on the reproducing population.

Ecologists will tell you that it's impossible to predict just how much havoc the Asian carp might wreak on the ecosystem of the Great Lakes, home to a $7 billion fishery; they will also tell you that we have more than carp to worry about. A 2011 report commissioned by the U.S. Army Corps of Engineers estimates that 87 species in the Great Lakes are at risk of invading the

Mississippi and another 57 are threatening to travel in the other direction. They have colorful names: the spiny water flea, the bloody red shrimp, the northern snakehead, the red-rim melania. Those numbers do not include the 103 other species—the round goby, the zebra mussel—for which, according to the report, "any dispersal control mechanism is already too late."

When dynamite and the steam-powered dredge breached the subcontinental divide in 1900, it also breached thousands of years of evolutionary history. Ecologists and political leaders in Great Lakes states downstream from Chicago argue that as long as the canal remains open, the invasions will continue. The best permanent solution, they say, is "hydroseparation." In other words, we need to part the waters, restore the continental divide.

In a much-anticipated report with a misleadingly bland title, "The Great Lakes and Mississippi River Interbasin Study," the U.S. Army Corps of Engineers recently affirmed the feasibility of hydroseparation but has yet to make a recommendation to Congress. Whatever recommendation it makes, the very prospect of reengineering the canal suggests something about the ways our geographies and our own out-of-scale place in them have changed.

"The canal is the only remaining link wanting to complete the most stupendous chain of inland communications in the world," one visitor to Chicago wrote in 1834. That use of the word "communications" sounds archaic to our ears, but there's a furtive meaning bottom-dwelling in those etymological channels. Ideas, goods, images, species—everything is communicable now. In shortening distances, we've accelerated processes—climatological, evolutionary—to a pace even our own species, the most adaptable, invasive one on the planet, is struggling to keep up with.

Don't ask just the ecologists. Ask the engineers. Increasingly, it's the consequences of our own past creations they're seeking to deliver us from. That recent report celebrates the Army Corps's "efforts to restore the natural characteristics of aquatic systems." Those efforts include "hydrologic regime reestablishment, dam removal, river meandering, reconnecting floodplains, reintroduction of fire, etc." More than 1,000 dams have been removed from American rivers in the past century, 72 of them in 2014 alone. Homesteaders drained wetlands; after Hurricanes Katrina and Sandy, we're building them. Battling the effects of climate change is now central to the Army Corps's mission. Having spent centuries trying to bring natural forces under our control, our civil engineers are now declaring peace with them, or at least establishing diplomatic relations.

It's enough to make you wonder if water might once again assume a place of prominence in our geographies, which is not to say that we should throw away our Global Positioning Systems and go back to using Joliet's hand-drawn navigation chart. No matter how accurate or beautiful, all of those old maps leave out a crucial dimension, one that computer models of planetary processes have only recently added to ours: time. On our best maps, the rivers move.

THE ZEALOT

Near the railroad tracks on the outskirts of Flint, Michigan, there is an old pump house, the walls of which have long served as a kind of communal billboard. The Block, people call it. They paint messages there—birthday wishes, memorials for the dead. In January of 2016, after Governor Rick Snyder declared a state of emergency in response to Flint's water crisis, a new message appeared, addressed implicitly to Snyder but also to the world: YOU WANT OUR TRUST??? WE WANT VA TECH!!! In the history of political graffiti, "We want Va. Tech" may sound like one of the least stirring demands ever spray-painted on a wall, but in the context of Flint, it was charged with the emotion and meaning of a rallying cry.

By "Va. Tech," the message's author meant a Virginia Tech professor of civil and environmental engineering, Marc Edwards. Edwards has spent most of his career studying the aging waterworks of America, publishing the sort of papers that specialists admire and the rest of us ignore, on subjects like "ozone-induced particle destabilization" or the "role of temperature and pH in $Cu(OH)_2$ solubility." Explaining his research to laypeople, he sometimes describes it as "the C.S.I. of plumbing." Edwards is a detective with a research lab and a Ph.D. In 2000, after homeowners in suburban Maryland began reporting "pinhole leaks" in their copper pipes, the water authority there brought in Edwards. In 2002, after receiving a report that water in a Maui neighborhood had mysteriously turned blue and was giving people rashes, Edwards took on the case.

Before Flint, the most famous case Edwards investigated was the lead contamination of the water supply in the nation's capital—still the worst such event in modern American history, in magnitude and duration. In Washington, lead levels shot up in 2001, and in some neighborhoods they remained dangerously elevated until 2010. Edwards maintains, and spent years working to prove, that scientific misconduct at the Environmental Protection Agency and the Centers for Disease Control and Prevention exacerbated the D.C. crisis. A congressional investigation culminated in a 2010 report, titled "A Public Health Tragedy: How Flawed C.D.C. Data and Faulty Assumptions Endangered Children's Health in the Nation's Capital." It confirmed many of his allegations, but the experience was for Edwards a decade-long ordeal that turned him into a reluctant activist—or as he prefers to say, "a troublemaker."

For television appearances, Edwards will put on a suit and tie, and the tie almost always bears a picture of some endangered animal: a giant panda, for instance, or a water buffalo. But on the morning we met, in his lab at Virginia Tech, he was dressed in a black track suit and a pair of running shoes—the uniform he prefers. At fifty-two, he has the youthful yet slightly skeletal good looks of an avid long-distance runner, which he is. "Before Flint, I was running fifty miles a week," he told me. "Now I'm down to twenty-seven." Running keeps him sane, he says, or at least saner than he would be otherwise. More than once during his investigations into D.C. and Flint, he wondered if he might be losing his mind.

"Before D.C.," he told me, "I think I was a normal professor." In the sciences, normal professors with tenure do not maintain websites on which they publish incriminating emails obtained under the Freedom of Information Act. Or habitually refer to unethical bureaucrats as "pathological lying scumbags." Or allude frequently to Orwell's *1984*, Arendt's *The Origins of Totalitarianism,* and Ibsen's *An Enemy of the People,* an 1882 political drama about polluted water contaminating the profitable baths in a Norwegian town. Of his fellow tenured scientists, a normal professor doesn't say things like "We are the greatest generation of cowards in history."

~

The poisoning of Flint can be traced to the moment on April 25, 2014, when, with the push of a button, the city stopped buying treated water from Detroit and began drinking from its own notoriously polluted river. In the year after the switch, the city violated the Safe Drinking Water Act four times—for increases in *E. coli,* coliform bacteria, and trihalomethanes, a class of carcinogenic "disinfection byproducts." The switch also probably contributed to an outbreak of Legionnaires' disease that killed at least twelve people. And for reasons that remain unclear, workers at Flint's hastily refurbished and understaffed treatment plant failed to add corrosion inhibitors, chemicals that coat the interior of pipes, providing a prophylactic barrier. Stop adding them, and the coating wears away, the pipes corrode, lead leaches into the water.

Edwards himself didn't discover the corrosive chemistry

of Flint's water. LeeAnne Walters, a mother of four, did that after her children broke out in rashes. In early 2015, Walters began investigating. A test conducted by the city at her request detected dangerously elevated lead levels in her tap water. After obtaining the list of chemical ingredients that the Flint treatment plant was using, Walters shared them with an E.P.A. drinking-water expert named Miguel Del Toral. Notably absent from the list: corrosion inhibitors. "I couldn't believe that they didn't have corrosion control," Del Toral told me. Untreated, nearly all water will corrode metal, but some water sources are more corrosive than others, and the water from the Flint River, Del Toral says, "was corrosive as hell." He had corresponded with Edwards before; now he had Walters collect water samples from her house and send them to Edwards's lab for analysis. In one sample, the lead levels were so high that the water qualified as hazardous waste.

In the summer of 2015, when Walters went public with an E.P.A. memorandum that Del Toral wrote and sent her, the Michigan Department of Environmental Quality tried to discredit it. In statements to reporters, a department spokesman, Brad Wurfel, called Del Toral "a rogue employee" and said Michigan officials had found no evidence of a citywide lead contamination. Wurfel's advice to Flint residents: "Relax." Walters, whose son had already received a diagnosis of lead poisoning, enlisted Edwards, who began conducting, with the help of Walters and other volunteers, what he claims was "the most thorough independent evaluation of water in U.S. history."

That September, at a news conference on the lawn of City Hall, encircled by activists, Walters by his side, Edwards announced what he had found: that lead levels in the tap water of "about 5,000 Flint homes" exceeded the safety standard— 10 parts per billion—of the World Health Organization. In October, the city switched back to Detroit water. In December, Flint's newly elected mayor, Karen Weaver, presented Edwards with a commemorative plaque. "We had cried out for a year and a half, and it wasn't until you came that you gave our voice some validation," she told him. "It wasn't until you came, and we got those Virginia Tech results, that we knew: People couldn't say we were crazy. They couldn't say we didn't know what we were talking about. They couldn't say it was our imagination."

Edwards's decision to champion the cause of activists is not one scientists typically make; they avoid political contro- versies for a reason. In 2011 the American Association for the Advancement of Science, the largest scientific society in the world, commissioned a paper on the "standards, benefits and risks" of advocacy. "When scientists become advocates, they become 'partisans' and are no longer neutral conveyors of sci- entific information," the paper stated. "While the line between neutral and partisan, between dispassionate and passionate, is not easily drawn, it nonetheless exists." Scientists who trans- gress that line tend to have their credibility impugned. Just ask the climatologists. Or think of Rachel Carson, who was a sci- entist with the United States Fish and Wildlife Service before she became an author. Upon the publication of *Silent Spring* in 1962, critics accused her of hysteria and Communism.

Consider the case of Clair Cameron Patterson, the geo- chemist who first determined the age of the planet from lead isotopic data. While working with that data, Patterson discovered, in the early 1960s, that scientists had grossly underestimated the amount of lead we were adding to the environment. There was lead in our gasoline, in our paint, in canned tuna, in our plumbing. The lead levels in the bodies of postwar Americans were 700 to 1,200 times as high as those of their preindustrial ancestors, Patterson estimated. For more than twenty years, the lead industry resisted his campaign to ban the metal from consumer products. The United States didn't remove the last of the lead from gasoline until 1996. Though our lead levels are still around 10 to 100 times as high as those of our preindustrial ancestors, they have, on average, been coming down ever since. But in 1965, when Patterson first began sounding the alarm about lead, prominent toxicologists dismissed him as a "zealot" who had abandoned science for "rabble rousing."

Edwards considers Patterson a role model. He would prefer to remain dispassionate, he says, but his experiences in D.C. and Flint taught him that neutrality carries its own risks. If, as surveys suggest, Americans are less willing to defer to the authority of scientific experts than they once were, scientists themselves are partly to blame, Edwards believes. In the academy, competition over a dwindling pool of funding and the pressure to publish have created "perverse incentives," he said in a recent interview with the *Chronicle of Higher Education*. As a result, "the idea of science as a public good is being lost," and along with it, the "symbiotic relationship" between the scientific community and the public. For him, his intervention in Flint was a kind of demonstration project, a case study of how to conduct science ethically, in the public sphere and for the public good.

Michigan officials initially tried to discredit him too, trotting out the rabble-rousing charge. Although the state "appreciates academic participation in this discussion," Wurfel, the Michigan Department of Environmental Quality spokesman, wrote in an email to a local reporter, "offering broad, dire public-health advice based on some quick testing could be seen as fanning political flames irresponsibly."

A scientist abiding the paper commissioned by the American Association for the Advancement of Science would have responded to Wurfel dispassionately, perhaps by conveying his data in a peer-reviewed journal. Instead, Edwards fought back like some twenty-first-century pamphleteer. On a website one of his graduate students built, flintwaterstudy.org, he posted, along with incriminating documents and helpful tips for Flint residents, acerbic commentaries condemning Wurfel and other officials he considered culpable. "You wish they'd listen to reason, scientific facts, the truth," he told me. "But if they're corrupt, the only weapon you've got is ridicule."

In Flint, Edwards's pugilistic brand of advocacy seemed to work. In December, Wurfel and other officials resigned. In February, Congress invited Edwards to testify at hearings devoted to the Flint crisis, and in a rare display of bipartisanship, Democrats and Republicans alike solicited his opinions not only on matters of science but also on matters of policy and morality and the law, treating him as a sort of oracle or ombudsman. It was hard to recall a scientist who had received a warmer reception on Capitol Hill. Governor Rick Snyder had by then acceded to the demand spray-painted on the Block, appointing Edwards to the task force overseeing the state's response to the emergency in Flint. The E.P.A. awarded Virginia Tech an $80,000 grant to retest the city's water. Edwards had done as much as anyone to expose the betrayal of public trust in Flint. Who better than him to restore it?

~

With his son and daughter, both teenagers, and his wife, Jui-Ling, Edwards lives at the border of a national forest, atop Brush Mountain, one serration in the Appalachian chain. They heat their three-story house entirely with firewood that Edwards scavenges from the forest, and they draw their water from a well. Throughout the house, Edwards keeps gym equipment strategically placed—dumbbells in his living room, a treadmill and barbells in the basement.

He grew up in Ripley, New York, a rural town on the shore of Lake Erie. As a teenager, he worked menial jobs, picking grapes in the local vineyards and cleaning rooms at a motel, saving for college. He attended SUNY-Buffalo, majoring in biophysics because it was reputed to be the hardest major, combining the curriculums of biology, physics, chemistry, and math. In his senior year, he applied successfully to the graduate program in civil engineering at the University of Washington, in Seattle. In his application's personal statement, he wrote that the restoration of Lake Erie, which he witnessed in the 1970s after the passage of the Clean Water Act, had given him his life's purpose: to improve "the future of water supplies."

The director of his dissertation at U.W. was an environmental engineer named Mark Benjamin. The two grew close, and have remained close, despite differences of temperament and politics. In the acknowledgments section of his dissertation, Edwards says of Benjamin, "I will do well to follow his sterling example in future professional activities, while at the same

time attempting to shake the aftereffects of his Stanford socialistic drivel."

"As you probably know, since you've spent a lot of time with
him, Marc has strong political views," Benjamin told me. It
was true. Edwards had made his political views clear. In Virginia, when I visited him, we had watched the returns of the
South Carolina presidential primaries together in his living
room, Edwards in gym shorts lifting twenty-seven-pound
weights. He is a Republican, a fiscal conservative with a libertarian bent, as well as an environmental-justice warrior. "The
crack about 'Stanford socialistic drivel' had become a running
joke by then," Benjamin says. "But absolutely there was more
than a grain of serious resentment at people feeling entitled by
having gone to the best schools, as the world sees those rank-
ings. Given his SUNY-Buffalo background, I'm sure he felt
disrespected."

Edwards and Benjamin believe that, adhered to rigorously,
the scientific method provides some protection from bias,
political or otherwise, and by all accounts Edwards is a brilliant
scientist. "Really, he's almost unique in the field right now, how
much he's admired," Benjamin says. Other scientists I spoke
to said the same, affirming the wisdom of the judges who in
2007 awarded Edwards a MacArthur Fellowship, the so-called
Genius Grant. (In its citation, the foundation praised him for
"playing a vital role in ensuring the safety of drinking water.")

Outside the realm of science, Edwards has strong differences of opinion with many of his admirers. In the written
statement he submitted with his congressional testimony, he
included a somewhat cryptic sentence. "While misconduct has
always been a problem, at some level, since the earliest days of

the scientific revolution," he wrote, "the rise of institutional scientific misconduct is a relatively new phenomenon."

When I asked him what he meant, he referred me to a 2014 book for which he wrote the foreword, *Science for Sale*, by David L. Lewis, an E.P.A. whistle-blower. Lewis defines "institutional scientific misconduct" as "the fraudulent manipulation of science by government agencies, corporations and academic institutions to support government policies and industry practices." In his foreword, Edwards commends Lewis but quibbles with his definition. It's the misconduct of public institutions, not private ones, that worries Edwards most. "In my opinion," he writes, "the abuses and dangers of institutional scientific misconduct," where no profit motive appears, "far exceed those arising from misconduct in industrial science."

Edwards's cynicism about the public sector was deeply shaped by the "D.C. saga," Benjamin told me. In Washington, when Edwards started leveling allegations against the E.P.A. and the C.D.C., he was treated by some as a pariah in his field, the scientist who cried "Lead!" in a crowded metropolis—or "the engineering equivalent," Benjamin says, "of an ambulance chaser."

Bruce Lanphear, a public-health physician who has studied environmental lead poisoning since the 1990s, shares Edwards's concern about the failures of regulatory agencies but attributes them mainly to the institution that invited Edwards to testify: Congress. He pointed out that in the last two decades Congress has cut the E.P.A.'s budget by 30 percent, even as the agency's regulatory mandates have increased.

"We're still using children as biological indicators for substandard housing," Lanphear says. "Everything is focused on short-term solutions, crisis thinking, the bottom line." The crisis in Flint has led to congressional hearings and criminal charges against nine Michigan officials but not yet to the kind of action Lanphear believes the nation needs to take. "Within the next thirty years, we're going to need to have replaced our entire water infrastructure," Lanphear says. "So what's the plan?"

~

That winter and spring, whenever Edwards went to Michigan, television cameras tended to follow. One morning, a team sent by RT, the Russian news network, trailed him to an elementary school—not in Flint but just outside it, in the comparatively affluent, predominantly white suburb of Grand Blanc. Joining Edwards on his classroom visit was Mona Hanna-Attisha, a pediatrician at Hurley Medical Center in Flint. Like many people in Michigan, she first heard of Edwards when he stepped before the television cameras in the summer of 2015. At the time, she was working on a study of her own, an analysis of pediatric blood data that would confirm what the Virginia Tech water study had implied—that blood-lead levels in Flint had shot up after the city seceded from Detroit's water system. Edwards had identified the cause, Hanna-Attisha the effect. She wasn't sure why state agencies had missed the blood-lead increase she had found. Trying to explain their failure, their collective blindness, she mentioned an aphorism she learned in medical school: "The eyes don't see what the mind doesn't know."

In a second-floor classroom, the pair sat in tiny red chairs, Edwards in an ill-fitting suit, Hanna-Attisha in an ankle-length parka, drinking cocoa from mugs and taking questions from small interrogators—the fourth-grade version of a congressional hearing. Edwards testified that something "governments don't do very well is fix the problems they create."

"Do you blame the government for what happened?" a boy in the front row asked.

"Yes, I do," Edwards said. "Did you pick up on that?"

Another child wanted to know what happens to officials who break the law.

Hanna-Attisha joked that they get a "timeout."

Edwards liked this. "A really bad timeout!" he said. All the grown-ups laughed.

"And everyone gets fired!" the boy in front said.

"We can also have stronger laws and stronger rules," Hanna-Attisha said once the laughter died down, "to prevent this from happening in other cities."

Grand Blanc and Flint have a tangled history. A half-century ago, during the days of white flight, General Motors executives pushed to combine suburbs and city into a single metropolis— New Flint—with shared government services and a shared tax base. In 1958, opponents in the suburbs blocked the plan. People in parts of Flint now have a life expectancy fifteen years lower than those in some neighboring suburbs, and even before the water crisis, children in Flint had higher blood-lead levels than their suburban counterparts. "Our Flint kids have every obstacle to success," Hanna-Attisha told me back at her office. "We have a forty-two percent poverty rate here; it's about 16 percent in the state. We have one of the highest crime rates. We don't have full-service grocery stores."

Flint's plight, in other words, predated the water crisis and would outlast it. At the time of Edwards's classroom visit, four months after Flint rejoined Detroit's water system, Edwards's research team and the citizen scientists who volunteered to assist it were preparing to resample the same 271 taps that Virginia Tech had originally sampled. The results would reveal how far lead levels had fallen. Knocking on doors, they encountered an unanticipated obstacle: Many of the occupants of those 271 homes had moved away, locking their doors behind them. Civil engineers refer to the time that water spends in pipes as "water age." Flint's loss of population meant that fewer people were opening their taps, which meant that Flint's water was getting older. The older the water, the longer it would take for corrosion inhibitors to work their way through all the pipes.

Of the 271 homes that Virginia Tech had tested, the lead levels in Elnora Carthan's house—1,050 parts per billion, 70 times as high as the E.P.A. limit—were the highest. When Edwards visited Carthan's tiny yellow bungalow in the spring of 2016, scraps of copper piping lay coiled in the grass, the remnants of the service line that a construction crew sent by the city had just ripped out. The crew was still there, putting a new copper service line in, threading it under the asphalt to the water main across the street.

"It's a big C.S.I.-of-plumbing case," Edwards said, "because why does she have so much lead but no lead pipe?" He crouched on the lawn, peered into a length of pipe, and blew into one end of it. Having found no clues, he tagged a few scraps to take back to his lab for further study.

In Carthan's basement, he inspected the plumbing with a flashlight. Traditionally, civil engineers have concerned themselves with public works, leaving household plumbing to plumbers. But in the 1990s, Edwards realized that the

distinction between private property and public works had
everything to do with legal liabilities and nothing to do with
chemistry. Legally, a homeowner is responsible for what happens after water crosses the property line, which is one reason water companies are keen to attribute lead poisoning to
household sources. But what happens to water at the municipal treatment plant, or on its subterranean journey, can have
unintended side effects within the home. Depending on its
chemistry, water can eat pinholes into copper pipes. It can turn
a basement water heater into an incubator of legionella or other
bacteria. And if its chemistry is corrosive, it can leach lead from
the solder or from brass faucets. Old plumbing fixtures made
of brass were often as much as 20 percent lead by weight, and
until 2014 even brass faucets advertised as lead-free could contain up to 8 percent lead by weight in the United States. Solder,
brass fixtures, or maybe a chunk of lead obstructing a pipe—
those, Edwards hypothesized, were the likely sources of the
lead in Carthan's water. To test his hypothesis, he hired a local
plumber for the day to replumb Carthan's house with PVC.
From her old plumbing, he collected samples and added them
to the heap of evidence destined for his lab.

Out in her driveway, Carthan stood by, watching the scientists at work. Born in Arkansas, she moved to Flint in 1976 and
had been there ever since, even though her children and grand-
children had all moved away. She herself had never drunk
the poisoned water or served it to guests. "When they first
switched," she said, "it had an odd smell. A really odd smell.
You knew something was wrong. You turn the shower on, and
you could smell it. You take a shower, five or ten minutes later,
you begin to itch. You knew there was something wrong. That's

why people were complaining. But nobody was listening"—
until Virginia Tech arrived. Carthan signed up to participate
in last summer's water study as soon as she heard about it.

Edwards credited much of the success of his intervention in
Flint to an anthropologist named Yanna Lambrinidou. Lambrinidou had helped organize a coalition of activists during
D.C.'s lead crisis. It was their work, and Lambrinidou's in particular, that brought his D.C. research to the attention of Congress, Edwards told me. Without her efforts, the congressional
investigation that vindicated him might never have happened.

Collaborating on the D.C. crisis, Edwards tutored Lambrinidou in the chemistry of lead corrosion. In turn, she taught
him about the value of "vernacular" knowledge and the ethical hazards of scientific hubris. For several years, Edwards and
Lambrinidou together taught a course at Virginia Tech called
Engineering Ethics and the Public, in which students studied cases of scientific misconduct and practiced ethnographic
methods—what Lambrinidou calls "learning to listen." In
Flint, Edwards told me, he tried to apply everything he had
learned from her.

Lambrinidou was at first reluctant to speak to me. Eventually, she explained why. Although she considered "Marc's con-
tribution in Flint and D.C. absolutely essential," on his website
and in the news media, Edwards had contributed to a simplistic
"hero narrative" about Flint. This was a complaint I heard from
other environmental-justice advocates—that Edwards had
cast himself, or been cast by the news media, as Flint's white
knight. A number of people I spoke to, Lambrinidou among
them, referred to a comment that Irma Muñoz, the president
of an advocacy group called Mujeres de la Tierra, had made at

a recent conference on citizen science: "We don't want our day saved," Muñoz said. "We want to save our own day."

Paul Schwartz, a water activist who worked with Edwards and Lambrinidou in D.C., told me there were times when Edwards "would be helpful and supportive, and there were times when he shoved us aside and inserted himself right into the middle of the story."

In an email to me, Lambrinidou wrote: "We are all capable of outstanding courage (even if at times we have been 'cowards') and of outstanding wrongdoing (even if at times we have been 'heroes'). This is what it means to be human, no? This is what it means to be a parent, a teacher, a doctor, a president. We all know that at times we've shined beyond even our own greatest expectations, and at times we've failed spectacularly to the point of self-shock. I think that Marc, not unlike many individuals and institutions embracing 'hero' narratives, struggles sometimes to hear this."

She described an alternative situation that might have played out in Flint, one she had seen play out in other collaborations between citizens and scientists. What if Edwards had stayed in Virginia, or at least away from the cameras? What if he had supported the activists in Flint with technical expertise but let them announce the findings of the study they conducted with his help? I wasn't sure. If LeeAnne Walters had presented the evidence on the lawn of City Hall instead of Edwards, would people outside Flint have taken the evidence as seriously?

～

In the spring of 2016, a new outsider began making trouble in Flint, the actor Mark Ruffalo, who founded an environmental group called Water Defense. Ruffalo had appointed a man named Scott Smith to serve as Water Defense's chief water scientist. When Smith went to Flint, he took what he called Water Defense WaterBugs, colorful sponges of "open-cell elastomeric foam technology." They looked like Koosh balls made from shredded swimming-pool noodles. Smith tossed them into the Flint River. He tossed them into bathtubs and shower stalls. In a video that Water Defense posted online, Smith claimed that the research carried out by others was fundamentally flawed, because it relied entirely on "grab samples" that collect "a split second" of water, and people don't "bathe for a split second." (In fact, Edwards says, Virginia Tech used an array of proven sampling methods.)

In April, at a meeting of the Flint City Council inside City Hall, Smith issued a warning that bore an uncanny resemblance to those Edwards had issued the previous September. "It is irresponsible and incomprehensible for anyone to declare or suggest that the water in Flint is safe to bathe or shower in," Smith said. No one had tested the showers and bathtubs of Flint for "the full spectrum of chemicals, including but not limited to chemicals that volatilize or aerosolize in the air and pose a direct inhalation risk into the lungs." It was a convincing performance, not only because Smith sounded scientific but also because his assessment helped explain symptoms that residents of Flint continued to report even after they stopped drinking the poisoned water—rashes, hair loss, difficulty breathing, a burning in the lungs. In February alone, there were so many complaints from Flint residents that state and federal public-health officials opened a new investigation.

"This is exactly the danger of having untrustworthy

government science," Edwards wrote me in an email. "A Hollywood fraud rolls into town, and they cannot even call him out." Concerned that Water Defense would scare even Flint residents who reported no adverse symptoms, he decided to go after Ruffalo and Smith the way he'd gone after government officials. "A-List Actor but F-List Scientist: Mark Ruffalo Brings Fear and Misinformation to Flint" read the headline of a blog post he published on flintwaterstudy.org.

"Not everyone who challenges the claims of the E.P.A., C.D.C. and State of Michigan are automatically correct," he wrote. Smith had no degrees in the sciences, Edwards noted, and appeared to be a businessman of dubious accomplishment who was now trying to market his sponges. Edwards made the case that Water Defense's meddling would do harm. A recent increase in gastrointestinal infections in Flint, Edwards speculated, could have been caused by the poor hygiene that Smith's "fear-mongering" had encouraged. The disinfection byproducts, or DBPs, that Water Defense had detected in showers—produced by reactions between chlorine and organic matter—had been reviewed by a scientist Edwards recruited, Dr. David Reckhow of the University of Massachusetts, Amherst, "one of the foremost authorities on DBPs in the world." Reckhow's assessment: "There is nothing at all unusual or abnormal in the Flint DBP data."

Water Defense, though, made its own appeal to authority. Smith was not a credentialed scientist, it was true, but all his samples were being tested by an independent lab and reviewed by Judith Zelikoff, a toxicologist in the environmental-medicine department at New York University. (Water Defense is "producing data in an ethical and transparent manner,"

Zelikoff told me, "and I will continue to support them.") Once again, Flint residents were left to wonder whom to believe.

This time, Edwards's pugilistic brand of advocacy proved less effective than it had the previous fall. Among the activists who fought to expose Flint's water crisis, a schism emerged. There were those, led by LeeAnne Walters, who kept faith in Virginia Tech, and those, led by another Flint mother, Melissa Mays, who placed their trust in Water Defense. Mays had helped conduct the fieldwork for the Virginia Tech water study and, like LeeAnne Walters, she appeared alongside Edwards at his news conference on the lawn of City Hall. Now, after his denunciation of Water Defense, she renounced him. "You aren't listening anymore," she wrote in an email that Edwards shared with me. "We'll go back to doing the work on our own with those willing to work WITH us in the community as we discover more and vindicate what the residents here already know by THE PAIN WE ARE IN, that it is not safe to bathe."

On a hot May afternoon, Mays and other Flint residents drove to Ann Arbor to protest outside the condominium on Main Street where Governor Rick Snyder lives when he isn't in Lansing. They wore bathrobes and carried signs calling for Snyder's impeachment. "Tricky Ricky, you can't hide! We can see your dirty side!" the protesters chanted. I spotted a woman in a pink bathrobe and a FLINT LIVES MATTER T-shirt whom Edwards had introduced me to in the winter. Her name was Nayyirah Shariff, and she was a community organizer with the Flint Democracy Defense League. When we first met, Shariff had expressed gratitude and admiration for what Virginia Tech had done, but her opinion of Edwards had since changed. "Now it feels like, intentionally or unintentionally, he's filling the role of the State of Michigan and how they felt about our experiences back in the summer of 2015."

When I caught up with Melissa Mays, she said, "What broke my heart the most is that when we brought Marc Edwards in last August, the state did the same thing to him, called him a fearmonger. That's the same thing that Marc just did to Water Defense." Edwards's remarks about hygiene, moreover, were offensive. People in Flint hadn't stopped bathing despite their adverse reactions. "You're saying that we're dumb and dirty," Mays said. "That's what's wrong with us."

~

At the end of May, Edwards returned to Michigan to hold yet another news conference, at which he and other scientists would try to allay the fears and doubts that Water Defense had fueled. For this occasion, Edwards toned down his rhetoric, presenting the latest data neutrally. Lead levels were still too high, but they were coming down. The disinfection byproducts were comparable to the national average. Sounding weary, he continued: "I understand that the trust will never be there for some people. If the residents in Flint, given their journey, decide they never want to drink tap water again, never want to take a bath or shower again, I'm not going to try to talk them out of it, because they went through hell for eighteen months."

After the news conference ended, Edwards visited the home of Mari Copeny, the nine-year-old known as Little Miss Flint, whose letter to President Obama prompted him to visit. From LeeAnne Walters, Edwards had learned that Water Defense had collected samples in Mari's home. She was at school, but her mother, LuLu Brezzell, let Edwards in. Even after the city returned to Detroit's system, the water gave her family bad rashes, Brezzell said. She showed him pictures—angry red splotches on hands and arms and legs. Washing the dishes made the skin on her knuckles blister and split. She and her children were still doing their best to practice good hygiene, but they had learned to take "speed showers"—no more than two minutes. Water Defense had found high levels of chloroform in her water. Another scientist, with Hydroviv, a company that sells water filters, told her that her chloroform levels were "comparable to other municipal water sources." Like many people in Flint, she didn't know what or whom to believe, but she was inclined to trust her symptoms and her senses. Her water smelled "like a swimming pool," and it had acquired a mysterious blue tint.

"So I do a lot of work with blue water all over the country," Edwards said. About 80 percent of blue-water cases are "natural," a trick of the light, he explained. In the remaining 20 percent, the tint comes from dissolved copper, and unlike lead, a little copper is harmless. To figure out whether Brezzell's blue water was natural or chemical, all you had to do was place a bottle of it and a bottle of store-bought water against a white background.

Upstairs in her little bathroom, he filled the tub. As the water rose, it took on a tint. "Can you see it?" Brezzell asked. "Nice and blue?"

"Oh, yeah, that's blue," Edwards said.

She was relieved to hear him say this. "People were saying: 'You're crazy. The water's not blue.' I'm like, 'Yes, it is!'"

"So now the question, though: Is it bluer than normal water?"

Edwards said. He performed his test, filling a bottle from Brezzell's tub and comparing it with a bottle of store-bought water.

"They're a different color!" Brezzell said hopefully.

Edwards held the bottles up to a fluorescent light above the sink. "That is blue water," Edwards said. "But it's light blue." He took the two bottles outside. In natural light, they were harder to distinguish. Compared with other blue water he had studied, on a blueness scale of 1 to 10, hers was low, around a 1.5, he estimated. He meant this to sound reassuring: The 1.5 was close to normal, most likely indicative of a little copper, but nothing to worry about.

"It's still darker, though," Brezzell said, and you could tell from the insistence in her voice that she was neither comforted nor convinced.

Edwards was not surprised by her reaction, he later told me. She had horrible rashes and so did her children. She was in pain. "And when you're in pain, you want an answer, even if it's wrong," and he had no firm conclusions to offer, only data and hypotheses. All he knew for certain was what the lab tests eventually told him: that contrary to what Water Defense had told her, the chloroform levels were typical for American cities. The same was true of the disinfection byproducts and copper. Her chlorine levels, though well below the E.P.A. limit, were a bit high. Perhaps this explained the rashes. Perhaps she and her children were sensitive to chlorine. Perhaps a filter for her shower head would help.

That August, a year after he'd first stepped before the television cameras in Flint, I spoke to Edwards one last time. The troublemaking outsider whom the authorities had accused of "fanning the political flames irresponsibly" was now the authority making that case about others, and if many of the activists considered him an untrustworthy agent of the state, there was nothing he could do about it. In both roles, he said, he had been the advocate for "sound science."

"This is what a 'dark age' looks like," he wrote me in an email the morning after our last conversation. "When science is no longer a source of enlightenment, people still need to believe in something." The people of Flint had been betrayed, and the betrayal had pushed some of them "into the anti-science camp." He continued: "We lost our authority and the public trust with good reason. After Flint kids were protected, I took off my activist suit and put on my lab coat. Some people assumed my motives could be changed just as easily. Not so, but arguing about it is not productive. Our energies have to be focused on not betraying the public in the first place."

MAMMOTH FEVER

In 1801, Charles Willson Peale, the curator of one of America's first museums of natural history, put a skeleton on display in Philadelphia's Philosophical Hall, setting off a popular craze—"mammoth fever," historians have called it. Trained as a painter, Peale was more showman than scientist, a precursor to P. T. Barnum as well as Neil deGrasse Tyson. (In fact, Barnum would later acquire much of Peale's collection.) Peale's beast was something of a chimera, a hybrid of anatomy and make-believe. In place of missing bones, he fashioned approximations out of wood and papier-mâché. In assembling it, he managed to aggrandize it. He stuck the tusks on upside down so that his beast resembled a walrus. In promotional material, he described it as "exclusively carnivorous." His bones, moreover, hadn't belonged to a mammoth at all but to its evolutionarily distant cousin, a species of prehistoric North American proboscidean that in 1806, five years after Peale put his specimen on display, the pioneering French naturalist Georges Cuvier would christen "le grande *Mastodonte*"—but never mind. Peale's skeleton was a hit, and it was mammoth, and not mastodon, fever that people caught.

There are signs we may be living through a second outbreak of mammoth fever. The remains of mammoths and their cousins keep emerging out of beanfields and permafrost, making headlines. They've also been making prominent cameos in books. A mammoth is the first of the seventeen animals Elena Passarello thinks eloquently about in her recent bestiary of essays, *Animals Strike Curious Poses*. Elizabeth Kolbert opens *The Sixth Extinction*, winner of the 2015 Pulitzer Prize, with a chapter on the paleontological case history of the mastodon.

One of Cuvier's contemporaries proposed calling the mastodon "the American *incognitum*." It's a shame the name didn't stick. Reading John J. McKay's *Discovering the Mammoth*, an unabridged version of the history Kolbert artfully condenses, one learns that for almost as long as they've been extinct, mammoths and their cousins have been to us figures of mystery, totems of the unknown, and invitations to fantasize about the past.

In China, people mistook dead mammoths for dead dragons. Ancient Greeks imagined they'd found the remains of Titans slain by the mutinous gods. Multiple villages in Sicily claimed to possess the remains of Polyphemus, the Cyclops blinded by Odysseus. (We now know that elephants once grazed on Sicilian hills. Look at a pachyderm skull, and you'll see that its nasal cavity bears some resemblance to the socket of an enormous eye.)

Across cultures and centuries, when imagining the distant past, people have tended to invent Golden Ages inhabited by beings who were, if not superior to us, then at least bigger. This may go some way toward explaining the 1801 outbreak of mammoth fever, whose victims included the newly elected president, Thomas Jefferson. A theory popular among European naturalists of the time held that the animals of North America, humans included, were "degenerate forms" of those found in the Old Country. For chauvinistic reasons, Jefferson loathed this theory, which insulted colonists and Native Americans alike, and in the mastodon he found his disproof. Like Peale, he couldn't resist aggrandizing the animal, describing it "as being six times the size of modern elephants and therefore far greater than anything found in the Old World." In case mastodons might still be out there, roaming the American West, Jefferson instructed Lewis and Clarke to look for them, which suggests that not only was Peale a precursor to Barnum; his beast was a forebear of King Kong.

One gets the impression that McKay, possessed by a kind of scholarly monomania, has hunted down every written reference to mammoths and mammoth bones ever made, and it is impressive how many authors ancient and modern expressed an opinion on the subject. As he stalks his quarry through the wilds of medieval treatises on, for instance, the disputed existence of giants, even readers who share his fascinations— with mammoths or with medieval treatises—may weary of the chase. Once he reaches the seventeenth century, when anatomists finally noticed the resemblance to elephants, McKay builds a persuasive case that the mystery of mammoths is one of the great detective stories in the history of science. Cuvier's comparative anatomical studies of these ancient pachyderms led him to his heretical discovery, announced in 1796, of the phenomenon of extinction. As evolution would a few decades later, extinction upset the old cosmologies.

Since Cuvier's time, paleontologists and geologists have identified with confidence five major mass extinctions—the Big Five, they call them. In *The Ends of the World*, accompa-

nying scientists and amateur fossil hunters into the field, seeking lost worlds at the edges of highways and parking lots, Peter
Brannen takes readers on a time-traveling tour through all
five, in chronological order. Throughout, he is a companion-
able guide, as good at breathing life into the fossilized prose of
scientific papers as he is at conjuring the Ordovician reign of
the nautiloids. Although a world-destroying asteroid can make
for a spectacular apocalypse, many of the most lethal events in
Earth's history, Brannen learns, have been homegrown.

Investigations into the Devonian Extinction, which around
400 million years ago terminated the Age of Fishes, have
recently pointed not to an asteroid, or a supervolcano, or any
of the usual cataclysmic suspects, but to an unexpected one:
trees. As they successfully colonized the continents, trees
sent roots into the rock, building soil that washed into the
ocean, fertilizing algal blooms of the sort that account for the
Gulf of Mexico's anoxic dead zones. Their leaves, meanwhile,
drew down carbon dioxide from the Devonian atmosphere—
enough, evidence suggests, to induce an ice age. In debates
about climate change, sophists like to observe that the Earth's
climate has changed wildly in the past, the implication being
that climate change is perfectly natural. That this is irrefutably
so should comfort no one. We're also perfectly natural, after
all. But if human activity does bring about yet another mass
extinction, we can at least console ourselves with the notion
that trees did it first.

Devonian trees, however, didn't know what they were doing
when they did it. And of course, we're not depleting carbon
dioxide. We're increasing it at "perhaps the fastest rate of any
period in the last 300 million years of earth history." The planet

has run greenhouse experiments before, and if we wish to know their results, we can follow the geologic record back 250 million years to the hell of the End-Permian, when temperatures in acidic oceans reached 104 degrees Fahrenheit and "hypercanes" blasted around the hemispheres. Hurricane Irma, we were told in 2017, was as big as Ohio. End-Permian hypercanes attained the magnitude of continents. There followed what paleontologists call the Great Dying, the worst extinction in the planet's history, which extinguished 90 percent of life on Earth. Amid all the eschatological gloom, Brannen does offer some hopeful news: However alarming, the extinction rate we've seen in the last four centuries does not come close to rivaling the Big Five—not yet.

Woolly mammoths turn up toward the end of Brannen's guided tour. As he reminds us, the animals vanished so recently it's still possible to eat mammoth meat pulled from the Arctic refrigerator. Paleontologists have by now mostly solved the mystery of the mammoth's disappearance—mostly, but not quite. The retreat of the ice sheets a dozen-odd millenniums ago likely played a role, but mammoths had survived interglacial warm periods before, by shifting latitudes. Why did they disappear this time? Along with beavers the size of bears? And sloths the size of elephants?

Brannen favors the overkill hypothesis—that spearchucking humans drove the mammoth, if not to extinction, then to extinction's brink. The case, among scientists, remains open, and hotly debated. Rivals to the overkill hypothesis include, among others, the landscaping hypothesis, according to which we eradicated mammoths by burning down their habitats. Amazingly, scientists not long ago discovered that a remnant mammoth population on Wrangel Island in the Siberian Arctic held on until just a few thousand years ago, but their gene pool was too small, and they succumbed to inbreeding, also known as genetic decay—which is how isolated populations today often meet their end.

If Ben Mezrich's *Woolly* is to be believed, mammoths may be returning someday soon to a tundra near you, resurrected by the necromancers of synthetic biology. Even if you don't live to see a mammoth in the flesh, the odds are excellent you will have the opportunity to see its computer-generated likeness. Mezrich wrote the book that became *The Social Network,* and the cover of *Woolly* announces that a movie adaptation is already on the way. The advertisement is almost unnecessary. The book reads like an extended movie treatment, or mammalian fan fiction inspired by *Jurassic Park.*

The real star of Mezrich's story isn't his eponymous mammoth but the Harvard geneticist George Church. Along with journalistic access, Church has furnished Mezrich with nine epigraphs and an epilogue. A leader of the Human Genome Project and a pioneer of synthetic biology, Church is well suited to the familiar role Mezrich casts him in, that of the wizardly genius. Church even possesses what Mezrich describes as a "billowing white beard." In photographs, the beard looks more woolly than billowing; like it would take a hypercane to billow it. Not so Mezrich's prose. In hagiographic reconstructed childhood scenes, Mezrich has a prepubescent Church already speaking like someone trying out lines for a TED Talk.

Although the subtitle promises a "true story," *Woolly* is, like Peale's beast, something of a chimera, a hybrid of journalism and science fiction. (One chapter narrates, from the point of view of a doomed baby mammoth, a scene set 3,000 years ago on Wrangel Island. Another narrates, from the point of view of a scientist, a scene set "four years from today.") If a mammoth ever emerges from Church's lab, it will likewise be chimerical, in the genetic sense of that word—not the clone of an individual mammoth but an approximation of one conjured out of synthetic DNA spliced, crisply, into the genome of an Asian elephant, the mammoth's closest living relative. It would be, in effect, an Asian elephant compelled to express several of the mammoth's distinctive genetic traits: frost-resistant hemoglobin, diminutive ears, woolly hair. Mezrich makes believe that this brave new Snuffleupagus will be stomping around by the next presidential term. Even optimistic proponents of the science behind his fiction predict a birthday that middle-aged hominids like me probably won't be around to celebrate.

Why make a pseudomammoth? Ostensibly, for ecological reasons. The most fascinating chapter in Mezrich's book might well be one he didn't write. It excerpts "The Wild Field Manifesto," by Sergey Zimov. A Russian geophysicist, Zimov has spent much of his career working to resurrect an ecosystem, the pasturelands of the Siberian tundra as they existed 14,000 years ago, before bipedal apes with a taste for megafauna came along. His motives aren't nostalgic. He isn't trying to turn back time or build a new Eden so much as he's trying to landscape the future. The "frozen soils of the mammoth steppe" are "the biggest natural source of greenhouse gases on the planet," and the permafrost has already begun to thaw. Snow insulates soil, and by trampling it in search of forage, big herbivores expose the permafrost to the air, lowering ground temperatures by as much as 40 degrees centigrade. "It is very hard to agree to reduce industrial carbon dioxide emissions," Zimov writes. "Reducing permafrost emissions is much easier."

Zimov doesn't really need a living mammoth to restore the mammoth steppe, however. In a demonstration project he calls Pleistocene Park, he's already introduced other big herbivores adapted to cold climates: moose, Yakutian horses, Finnish reindeer, North American bison, elk, musk oxen, yaks. The greatest benefit that a mammoth might bring is publicity. Already, it is becoming to "de-extinction" what the humpback whale was to marine conservation four decades ago—a charismatic mascot. Save the Whale, Make a Mammoth.

It would be fitting and a touch ironic if we brought the mammoth back purely so that we could see a living, breathing one with our own eyes at long last. As Peter Brannen notes, the secret to the predatory success of our clawless, fangless species on the ice-age hunting grounds may well have been our culture—language, tools, art, all of those technologies that allowed us to acquire knowledge and transmit it across time. As John McKay informs us, paleontologists finally learned what mammoths looked like—the upward curling tusks, the humped shoulder, the downward-sloping spine—not by studying bones but by looking closely at ice age art made by those who'd observed the animals attentively, perhaps even lovingly, or wondrously, or worshipfully. Of the 255 engravings and paintings left by Paleolithic artists on the walls of the Rouffignac Cave in southern France, 16 depict the horse, 29 the bison. There are 11 rhinos, 6 snakes, 4 human figures, a single bear. The woolly mammoth outnumbers them all, recurring over and over, 158 times, like a dream.

FOUR LIGHTS

Evan S. Connell

On January 10, 2013, news came that one of the most singular careers in American letters had reached its last full
stop. Evan S. Connell was found in his Santa Fe apartment,
dead at the age of eighty-eight. He died alone, attended, one
presumes, by the "cracked Old Mexican pots and mutilated
statuettes" he collected—which is also how he lived and how
he wrote: apart from his contemporaries, in the company of
antiquities, as if he did not entirely belong to his time.

He twice traveled solo around the globe. In his writing, he
roamed across continents but also across centuries. Time—its
obliterating passage—was his great subject. It's there at the
very beginning, in the title story of the first book, *The Anatomy
Lesson and Other Stories,* published in 1957, when Connell was
thirty-three. The art professor who delivers the eponymous
anatomy lesson shows his students a Rembrandt portrait of a
young woman: "He told them that some afternoon they would
glance up by chance and see her; then they would know the
meaning of Time—what it could destroy, what it could not."
We hear that note again in Connell's debut novel, *Mrs. Bridge,*
published in 1959. In Chapter 45, titled "The Clock," the novel's

heroine seeks refuge in a stasis she mistakes for permanence: "Time did not move. The home, the city, the nation, life itself was eternal; still she had a foreboding that one day, without warning and without pity, all the dear, important things would be destroyed." We hear the note again four decades later, in the epigraph of *Deus lo Volt!*, Connell's chronicle of the Crusades, published in 2000: " 'The stream of Time, inexorable, constant,' wrote the Byzantine princess Anna Comnena, 'removes from our sight all things that are born, and carries into the night deeds of little account, deeds worthy of notice.' "

Although Connell innovated audaciously with prose forms, he did so in order to renew rather than resist the realist tradition. He remained devoted to Rembrandt, and in all of his wildly various books, he practiced a kind of life drawing. Witness *Mrs. Bridge*. Asked about the novel's unconventional, mosaic structure, he once said: "I had tried a traditional narrative, but found that this story, as is true with most of our lives, had no dramatic climax. Mrs. Bridge's life was one incident after another. There was not one great, explosive event, so I had to break it down into smaller moments." These moments are related to one another, but not, as the events in a narrative usually are, by cause and effect, and unlike most heroines, Mrs. Bridge does not develop as a character. Instead, what changes—deepens, complicates, accumulates pathos and meaning—is Connell's portrait of her.

Connell could be a merciless social critic, though he preferred the X-Acto knife of the ironist to the well-ground axe, and in his best work he combines irony with pity, often swerving without warning between the two. Early in *Mrs. Bridge*, many of the miniature chapters end with a punch line at the heroine's expense. As time passes, however, the jokes become less comic, more tragic; satire gives way to quiet desperation, which exhausts itself into elegy. In the penultimate chapter, ironically titled "Remembrance of Things Past," with Mr. Bridge dead and the children gone, what Mrs. Bridge dreaded has come to pass. The "dear, important things" have been lost, and she searches and searches for them in vain in the family photo album, which presents a kind of counternarrative to the album of moments Connell has assembled. (Kodak moments are not Rembrandt moments.) Snapshots of family vacations and birthday parties offer her a vision of a vanished past—a vision wishful and unreal.

Midway through his career, Connell turned from fiction to fact. Out of details he'd scavenged in archives, he did for historical figures—explorers, alchemists, pilgrims, crusaders—what he'd done for Mrs. Bridge. In the title piece of *The Aztec Treasure House,* his collected essays, he describes an Olmec statuette. "There can be no doubt that this was a person," he writes,

> not a symbol of humanity but a representative of it who lived in the area at that time, who sat cross-legged in the shade of a tree or in some thatched-roof hut while one of his neighbors manipulated the dark clay with a little stick, paused to stare, and tried again and then again in order to get the mouth just right, and the thrust of the nose, and the contour of the cheek, all for the sake of true expression.

The Aztec Treasure House is a cabinet of wonders, but Connell's nonfiction masterpiece, the book that along with *Mrs. Bridge* is likeliest to last, is *Son of the Morning Star,* an epic narrative history of the Battle of Little Bighorn. It's hard to imagine a character who would have less in common with the cavalry officers and Sioux warriors whose portraits Connell draws in *Son of the Morning Star* than Mrs. Bridge. And yet both books are time capsules of sorts, narratives that rescue "deeds of little account" and "deeds worthy of notice" from the wreck of time.

Connell's least classifiable books, written as he was making the transition from fiction to fact, take the form of notes collected by a prophetic, time-traveling wanderer. There are two of them, published a decade apart, *Notes from a Bottle Found at the Beach at Carmel* and *Points for a Compass Rose*. "The poetry of fact" is how Annie Dillard described them in a review. What she says of Connell's time-traveling note-taker applies equally well to Connell himself. "The speaker's ultimate role—his mission and his penance," Dillard writes, "is to exalt the suffering fragments of time and submit them to the healing glance of eternity."

One last quote, from one of the lesser-known novels, *The Connoisseur.* The book's protagonist, an insurance salesman named Muhlbach who lives in Westchester, is a recurring character in Connell's work and something of an authorial alter ego. Like his creator, Muhlbach is a collector—a connoisseur—of pre-Columbian artifacts. His connoisseurship begins on a business trip to New Mexico, when he visits an antiquarian's shop in Taos and discovers there a little terra-cotta chieftain carved by some Mayan sculptor centuries ago. The mutilated statuette casts a spell.

"How would it feel to be an artist," Muhlbach wonders, "to spend one's life observing the earth and the things that grow on it and attempting to communicate those observations? Take that little clay personage—how skillfully executed, how sensitive. How profoundly endowed with a knowledge of humanity its creator must have been."

Marilynne Robinson

Recently, visiting family, I spent some time leafing through one of those ancestral histories that Americans in rootless moods feel compelled to write. The manuscript was typewritten, handbound, homespun. Its author, a late great-uncle of mine, had been a public school teacher and administrator. From him, I learned that some of my forebears came to the American Midwest in the nineteenth century not only for the reasons I'd assumed—the arable soil offered to European immigrants by the Homestead Act, the freedoms of speech and religion. They also came for the schools, education having been in their corner of the Old Country a scarce resource, available to the few, withheld from the many.

I don't know how much to trust my great-uncle's account. He may have been seeking in the past the seeds of his own biography, as authors of such volumes are prone to do—as all of us, I suspect, are prone to do. And yet it's true that the American Midwest, in the century after Jefferson purchased it from Napoleon, provided unusually fertile soil for schools as well as corn. Just how fertile, Americans seem to have forgotten of late, and in her fifth collection of essays, Marilynne Robinson is here to remind us—of the Midwest's intellectual and political heritage, of the public university's democratic and humanistic origins, and of much else.

As novelist and essayist both, Robinson has always been something of an underwater archaeologist, diving into the twilight zones of memory to drag lost histories into the light. "I am especially fascinated by erasures and omissions, which seem to me to be strongly present in their apparent absence, like black holes, pulling the fabric of collective narrative out of shape," she writes here. It's worth pausing a moment over that metaphor to note how indebted it is to Melville and Dickinson and the Transcendentalists, whose influence Robinson has long welcomed and acknowledged. Like them, she is an ardent armchair naturalist, not to mention an ardent armchair theologian, cosmologist, ethicist, historian. Like them, she sees, or creates through metaphor, correspondences across disparate fields, frames of reference, states of being—between cosmos and mind, or astronomy and history, black holes and the absences in stories. Her way with metaphor implies a metaphysics, in her case a metaphysics informed by her Calvinism: History is a fabric. So is the cosmos. So are the moments lived quietly beside a mountain lake in Idaho, or in a prairie town in Iowa. Or on a whaling ship. Or wherever you are now. "What are all these fragments for," asks Ruth, the narrator of *Housekeeping*, Robinson's first novel, "if not to be knit up, finally?"

In her fiction Robinson knits narratively; in her essays rhetorically, inquisitively, at times polemically, but rarely autobiographically. Some writers moving between fiction and nonfiction are like musicians switching instruments. You can hear the difference when they put down one and pick up another, but the music, or the voice, is recognizably the same. Not so with Robinson. Readers who come to her essays having fallen under the spell of her fiction are likely to feel disoriented.

There is a dreamlike intimacy to the voices that narrate her novels, as if we were not so much listening to a story being told as eavesdropping on a consciousness. In *Gilead*, she gives us the diaristic letters of Reverend Ames, not his sermons. The voice of her essays, by contrast, seems to speak from a podium or pulpit. The difference between her fiction and nonfiction is akin to the one between practice and theory, or between a swim in a mountain lake and a lecture, delivered with unexpected brio and occasional thunder, on the properties of water.

In fact, all but one of the essays in the latest collection began as talks Robinson gave between the spring of 2015 and the spring of 2017, mostly at universities. In the middle of this lap around the lecture circuit, she published her fourth collection of essays, *The Givenness of Things*. It is perhaps not surprising that the talks she gave drew upon that book, sometimes heavily, or that in them she would sometimes repeat herself, repurposing the same material or ideas for different audiences. Nor is it surprising, given their dates of composition, that these new essays speak to our current historical and political moment. Robinson likes books that address "the Great Questions," and the title of the new collection, *What Are We Doing Here?*, asks several such questions at once, some ontological (Why do we exist?), some ethical (How should we act?). By *we*, Robinson sometimes means all of humanity; by *here*, she sometimes has in mind the universe. But *we Americans* are the portion of humanity that preoccupies her most.

She has become a kind of prophet and exegete of American democracy, as devoted to our secular scriptures as to her Christian ones. Her essays self-consciously recall the reformers of the nineteenth century, those Ciceros of the lyceum and the revival tent—a number of whom she has rescued from obscurity or disrepute, giving the Second Great Awakening its due for spreading abolitionism into the Free-Soil Midwest. Already in *When I Was a Child I Read Books* (2012), my favorite of her collections, Robinson was troubled by Donald Trump's forerunners, self-described patriots who sought to restore an American past that never was, dismissing as un-American values and institutions—public welfare, public education, religious pluralism—whose roots run back to Plymouth Rock. Her eloquence includes a gift for aphorism. Of our prejudices against the Puritans, she writes: "Stigma is a vast oubliette."

For all of their polarized divisiveness, Americans today have more in common than they commonly think, she contends, but this is no cause for celebration. Those on the Marxist left and the free-market right may imagine themselves to be ideological enemies, and yet both camps place their faith in an economic determinism that diminishes human complexity. Creationists and New Atheists, likewise, deserve each other. She sees in both a smug certitude whose source and symptom is a gross simplification of both the Bible and reality. "Complexity" and "mystery" are the magnetic poles Robinson navigates by, primary sources the water she swims in, "reductionism" the recurring object of her contempt.

At a time when academia can resemble an archipelago, the disciplines more specialized than finch beaks in the Galápagos, Robinson's audaciously heterodox thinking can exhilarate. She makes one wish that more literary scholars read up on dark matter, and that more professors in the STEM fields appreciated the difference between a mass spectrometer and a metaphor, the poetic logic of Genesis and a data set. Nevertheless,

Robinson is at her best when drawing upon her own reservoirs of learning in theology, history, and literature to fill in the omissions of others. When she aims polemically at certain of the sciences, or at modern and postmodern thought, her narratives create their own black holes.

She would have us remember that the colonists of Massachusetts Bay did not only hang witches and exterminate brutes; that they were, by historical standards, and by comparison to their brethren in Virginia, egalitarians who prized the freedoms of conscience over adherence to dogma; that their legal code was the ancestor of the Bill of Rights. And yet, by quoting selectively and misleadingly from *The Descent of Man*, she has in the past reduced Darwin, for instance, to a protoeugenicist, the fountainhead of social Darwinism, which is not unlike blaming John Calvin for the animatronic dinosaurs in the Creation Museum's diorama of Eden. Here, she asserts that Darwin's twenty-first-century successors in genetics and neuroscience would "annul the self as an intelligent moral actor." Surely, even a godless, literal-minded neuroscientist can marvel along with Robinson at the mystery of consciousness, and Darwin himself held that "of all the differences between man and the lower animals, the moral sense or conscience is by far the most important."

What most distinguishes this new collection from its predecessors is its sustained defense—spread across several essays but mounted most forcefully in "The American Scholar Now," whose title pays homage to Emerson—of the public university. Academics in the humanities have learned to portray their disciplines as delivery systems for marketable job skills. It is not inaccurate, that portrait. Those skills are real, as Robinson knows, especially in an economy that traffics so promiscuously in language and image. And she has noted, rightly, that "education is associated with prosperity," and that America's geopolitical ascendance coincides with the rise of the public university. But she resists these utilitarian concessions to the marketplace, for they entail yet another reduction of what it means to be both human and American, turning academia into a service industry, students into consumers and vocational trainees, education into a cost-benefit analysis from which even the STEM fields are no longer immune.

America's public universities were founded, Robinson notes, to democratize privilege—the privilege to prepare for a profession, yes, but also to learn how others over the course of history have answered the Great Questions, and how to ask and answer such questions for one's self. In some corners of the Old Country, literacy itself had been a privilege, and it remained one in the antebellum South. Robinson spent the last three decades on the fiction faculty at the Iowa Writers' Workshop. From our collective amnesia, she rescues her own university's origins. "What would early nineteenth-century settlers on the open prairie do first?" she asks. "Well, one of the first things they did was found a university, which is now about one hundred seventy years old."

She prefers eloquence and close reading to statistics, but here some are, adjusted for inflation: Between 1980 and 2017, the combined tuition and fees at four-year public colleges increased on average 319 percent. Between 2007 and 2016, meanwhile, state spending per student declined nationwide by 18 percent. To compensate for these austerities, students and their families have taken on more debt, and public institutions have had to entice more out-of-state and international students able to pay full fare. In the name of antielitism and economic populism, legislatures have helped make state colleges and universities more exclusive, not less. "History," as Robinson has said, "is a great ironist."

While reading *What Are We Doing Here?* I kept thinking of, in addition to my great-uncle, the students I teach at a public university in Detroit, many of whom are the first in their families to attend college, a large portion of whom are first- or second-generation Americans, many of whom observe a faith, many of whom do not, some of whom are majoring in the sciences, some in the humanities, nearly all of whom are anxious about their oncoming futures but nevertheless wish to study what we in the English department have to teach, having already gathered that although "it is difficult to get the news from poems," as William Carlos Williams wrote, "men die miserably every day for lack of what is found there." I also kept thinking of my grandmother, who like Robinson was a mainline Protestant. Born and raised by the agrarian floodplains of the Mississippi just south of St. Louis, the granddaughter of farmers and daughter of a mechanic in a tire factory, she was herself a first-generation college student, thanks to a scholarship from the University of Illinois. For her, church and university were both sources of meaning and community, equally sacred, equally American. "This country is in a state of bewilderment that cries out for good history," Robinson writes here—to which I can imagine what my grandmother might say, were she alive and seated in the lecture hall. The same thing I would say, though I left the church long ago: Amen.

Matthew Power

He was reporting on an explorer who is walking the length of the Nile when he was overcome by the heat and died, presumably of heatstroke, his wife, Jessica Benko, said.

—*"Matthew Power, Wide-Roving Journalist, Dies at 39"*
New York Times, *March 14, 2014*

January 1998. In the offices of a venerable magazine, I meet this hippie dude from Vermont: ponytail, spectacles of the sort favored by engineering students, lumberjack shirt. Matt Power. Others who've written remembrances of Matt have remarked on the poetry of his surname. In the spring of 1998, his fellow editorial interns treated it as if that were a thing—Matt power. If you had Matt power, you could recite entire episodes of *The Simpsons* by heart, along with passages from *Moby-Dick*. You could get yourself photographed by the *New York Times* while up a tree across from City Hall, protesting the closure of a community garden, wearing some sort of goofy sunflower headdress—some sort of goofy sunflower headdress and that goofy grin, goofy but also beautiful and disarming, scrolling upward into impish fiddleheads at the corners.

If you had Matt power, you could take up with a bunch of squatters in a derelict building in the South Bronx, as Matt did the year after we met. For some reason, I've always pictured him camped out on the building's roof, hanging his flannel underwear out to dry on a telephone wire, perhaps, or roasting a pigeon on a spit.

For all of his brainy bookishness and street smarts, Matt in the spring of 1998 was a greenhorn. We all were, but there was an innocence about him, some portion of which he never lost. I was only two years older, twenty-six to his twenty-four, which at the time seemed like a big difference and now seems like nothing. The rest of us were precociously world-weary, whereas Matt would never weary of the world.

I'll be honest, cooped up together day after day in the windowless room the interns shared, Matt sometimes got on my nerves. *Enough with* The Simpsons *already! Take a shower! See anyone else around here with a ponytail?* In May, when our internship was nearing its end and we were all frantically hunting for jobs, I called Matt from another room and introduced myself as Peter Canby, director of *The New Yorker*'s fact-checking department, to which Matt had submitted a résumé, and he fell for it, my Peter Canby act. And afterward, he grinned, a bit sheepishly, but he was crestfallen. I only remember that prank because years later, Matt would remind me, grinning and shaking his head, delighted now, "Remember when you pretended to be Peter Canby? Man, I totally fell for that."

He fell for it not because he was gullible, I think, but because he believed unquestioningly that his talents were commensurate with his dreams. Why shouldn't *The New Yorker* be calling? And he was right, his talents were commensurate with his dreams, which says something, considering the grand implausibility of his dreams.

A week after learning of his death, I happen to be teaching *The Songlines* by Bruce Chatwin, a writer I first read at Matt's recommendation, and rereading the book, which is at its heart an essay on "the nature of human restlessness," I keep thinking of Matt. Paraphrasing Pascal, Chatwin asks,

Why "must a man with sufficient to live on feel drawn to divert himself on long sea voyages? To dwell in another town? To go off in search of a peppercorn?" I would like to know Matt's answer.

Since his death, people have been asking me if Matt and I were close, and I don't hesitate to say yes, but our closeness was more a matter of time than place; it was the closeness of accumulated history. I never lived in Brooklyn, so I visited the house on Hawthorne Street less often than other friends of Matt and his wife, Jess. He and I were close because we'd set out together with a sense of common purpose. We'd known each other when we were both lowly greenhorn interns and when our careers as writers were still fantasies, and then slowly, arduously, luckily, separately but in tandem, competing with each other and cheering each other on, we'd acted those fantasies out and made them real. I never traveled with Matt on one of his expeditions, but since meeting him in 1998, I've always felt that I was traveling with him on the grand adventure of our lives.

~

A scientist I once wrote about told me that there are two kinds of oceanographers: those who go to sea and those who go to the lab. The same tends to be true of writers. Matt was unambiguously the former sort, and for a long while, I suspected I was doomed to be the latter. I reconciled myself to the editorial office and the classroom, enviously following Matt's seafaring from afar.

In 2007, during my last semester as a high school English teacher, I emailed Matt to invite him to visit my twelfth-grade literary journalism course. "Greetings from the Galapagos," he replied. "I'm here working on a couple of stories (just sailed across from Panama), and am flying tomorrow to Quito for a week and then back to NYC on the 18th. I'd be delighted to talk to your class." He came on a spring afternoon in early May. Having long since lost the ponytail and traded the woodsman's getup for a blazer of chestnut suede, face tan from his voyage to the Galápagos and grizzled with a day or two of stubble, he cut a dashing figure.

He'd recently published what remains one of my favorite pieces of his, "The Magic Mountain: Trickle-down Economics in a Philippine Garbage Dump," and I'd assigned it to my students. The subtitle suggests to readers that we may be in for a dreary trip. We are, and we aren't. There's a reason that the word "magic" appears in the title. Matt was an alchemist.

He begins in a traffic jam in Quezon City, on his way to Payatas, a fifty-acre dumpsite where, in July 2000, torrential rains set off an avalanche that buried alive the inhabitants of a shantytown who'd eked out something approaching a living by scavenging in the trash heap that buried them. Throughout his opening section, Matt makes the colossal landfill loom, the way the whale does in the opening chapter of *Moby-Dick*, building to this crescendo of images:

> As we come over a rise, my first glimpse of Payatas is hallucinatory: a great smoky-gray mass that towers above the trees and shanties creeping up to its edge. On the rounded summit, almost the same color as the thunderheads that mass over the city in the afternoons, a tiny backhoe crawls along a contour, seeming to float in the sky. As we approach, shapes and colors

emerge out of the gray. What at first seemed to be flocks of seagulls spiraling upward in a hot wind reveal themselves to be cyclones of plastic bags. The huge hill itself appears to shimmer in the heat, and then its surface resolves into a moving mass of people, hundreds of them, scuttling like termites over a mound. From this distance, with the wind blowing the other way, Payatas displays a terrible beauty, inspiring an amoral wonder at the sheer scale and collective will that built it, over many years, from the accumulated detritus of millions of lives.

A terrible beauty—the phrase captures so much of what Matt wrote.

Also characteristic of what he wrote is the way he refuses to let those people remain "a moving mass." Another passage:

We walk across a narrow bamboo bridge and up a steep hill, where a group of people—mothers with babies, men with arms crossed—sit in the shade of a military-style tent, in which a cooking class is under way. At the foot of the hill lies a half-acre of vegetables: beautifully tended rows of lettuce, tomatoes, carrots, squash, corn. A few people rest under a giant star-apple tree by a small creek. A pregnant woman with a little boy works her way down a row of tomato plants, pulling weeds. Tropical butterflies flit about. It would be an utterly rural and bucolic scene if it weren't for the rusty jumble of houses that begin at the field's edge, towered over by the gray hill of Payatas. The rumble of the bull-dozers and the trucks circling the road up its side is a dull grind, and periodically a plastic bag caught in an updraft drifts toward us and descends, delicate as a floating dandelion seed, into the branches of the trees.

There is so much about this passage that I admire, but above all what I love is how it brings together—or rather, keeps together—the natural and the human. They are inseparable, Matt knew. These few sentences, mostly descriptive, imply a philosophy, one that can register the resemblance between a plastic bag and a dandelion seed, one that can discover a garden in a wasteland, one that can reconcile that grin of his with the sense, as he wrote in "Holy Soul," that "at the core of life" is "sorrow and transience."

In my classroom on the afternoon that Matt visited was a student who would go on to become a reporter for the *New York Times*, and on the day I learned of Matt's death, this former student sent me a message about "The Magic Mountain." He wrote: "Remembering fondly the 'constellation fallen to earth' line you flagged for us, what, 8 years ago? What a kicker." I knew the line he was talking about, from the closing paragraph:

> At the open window the equatorial darkness falls like a curtain, and across the creek the mountain of the dumpsite rears black beneath a net of stars. Against the silhouette of the garbage mountain, a faint line of lights works its way upward. They are the homemade headlamps of the night shift tracing their way up the pile. Reaching the top, they spread themselves out, shining their lights on the shifting ground to begin their search. Beneath the wide night sky those tiny human sparks split and rearrange, like a constellation fallen

to earth, as if uncertain of what hopeful legend they are
meant to invoke.

Rereading that passage today, I find it hard not to think of all
the pictures of Matt wearing a headlamp, as if he were among
those fallen stars, those tiny human sparks, uncertain of the
legend he meant to invoke but certain somehow that it was a
hopeful one.

~

Shortly after Matt visited my class, I stopped teaching high
school English and set out to become, like him, the sort of
writer who goes to sea. In 2010, back in the "insular city of the
Manhattoes," once again pent up in lath and plaster, clinched
to a desk, I would become Matt's editor, and that experience
drew us closer still. At its best, the relationship between writer
and editor is deeply intimate, akin to that between athlete and
coach, or actor and director. Although I left editing before he
finished it, the last piece I assigned to Matt was a story about
urban explorers, and when he told me of his plan to go moun-
taineering on Notre Dame, I said to him something like, *Please
be careful, don't do anything stupid,* feeling that his life was in
my hands while also hoping, as editors do, that he would pull
it off, because how great would that be? A scene from atop
Notre Dame?

A year before he died, I moved to Michigan. We emailed
each other often, and whenever I returned to New York, I could
count on a drink with Matt. I think his thoughts, increasingly,
were turning toward shore. In his emails, the dreams he shared
were more sedentary than those he'd shared in the spring of

1998. In our last conversation, conducted by email but at the pace of conversation, a few weeks before his death, we talked about book projects. I had a notion of how he could turn one of his magazine stories, "Mississippi Drift," into a book. "This is the tricky part," I concluded my message. "You spend at least a couple of reclusive years saying no to magazine assignments unless they're somehow related so you can write the fucker." And he wrote back: "Well, next time you're in town, the whiskey's on me and we can hash out the details."

When I was first preparing to go to sea, I emailed Matt, asking for gear recommendations. He sent me an excellent packing list, which I'm now passing on to anyone else who wishes to go off in search of a peppercorn. His last piece of advice is the most essential:

hey Donovan,

a few things I've found indispensible:

Pelican laptop case. www.pelican.com Rock solid, waterproof, dustproof, padded on the inside. War correspondent's choice. It's heavy and expensive, but it's a tank.

A digital flash recorder. Great for interviews. You can download directly into a computer. You can alter the play-back speed so you can transcribe while you type. 12 hours recording time. About a hundred bucks. If you're recording a lot of interviews, I would absolutely get one.

A good umbrella is probably the most useful thing in the world, even when trekking. Golite makes some awe-some sturdy and lightweight travel umbrellas.

a leatherman multitool is great.

A universal adapter (switches between pretty much every bizarro form of outlet in the world.)

An LED headlamp (petzl and black diamond make great ones) is a must.

Cotton kills. You want layers of things like capilene and fleece with a good raincoat. My understanding is that goretex does not work in alaska, so you might need a proper maritime foul weather raincoat if you are going to be out on a boat in the bering strait or something.

Dramamine, bonine, ambien and a wide assortment of headache pills are always nice for plane trips/boat trips.

Walther PPK 9mm with hollowpoint rounds. Because you never know. Or if you really want that grizzly-stopping power, .357 and higher.

Bullwhip and fedora optional.

Keeping all this in mind, traveling light is nice.

Stay hydrated, I'll send more thoughts as they come along.

yrs

Matt

In penance for having teased him those many years ago, I'll end by doing what he might have done those many years ago—quote Melville: "Terrors of the terrible! Is all this agony so vain? Take heart, take heart, O Bulkington! Bear thee grimly, demigod! Up from the spray of thy ocean-perishing—straight up, leaps thy apotheosis!"

Henry David Thoreau

> Unsurprisingly, this thoroughgoing misanthrope did not
> care to help other people.... Poor Thoreau. He, too, was
> the victim of a kind of shipwreck—for reasons of his own
> psychology, a castaway from the rest of humanity.
>
> —*"Pond Scum," Kathryn Schulz,*
> The New Yorker, *October 19, 2015*

In a prominent national magazine, there appeared an indictment of the late Henry D. Thoreau, whose literary stock the
indictment's author judged to be grossly overvalued. It wasn't
just Thoreau's writing that deserved a take-down; so did the
man himself, if in Thoreau's case one could even distinguish
between the two. Thoreau was conceited, indolent, egotistical. Also: a failure, selfish, self-involved, useless, unimagi-
native, provincial. The indictment compared Thoreau to
Montaigne—unfavorably; called him a sophist, a hypocrite, a
humorless boor.

He'd spurned humanity's company, preferring "the society
of musquashes," and therefore didn't know anything about
the mass of men and their quiet desperation. He was a narcis-
sist who looked out at the world and saw his own reflection.
He had an unhealthy mind but went about prescribing medicine to others. He was forever nattering on about getting away
but remained close to home his entire life. The world did not
esteem him as highly as he esteemed himself. The world's low
esteem for him could be measured by the low sales figures of
his books. True, Thoreau could turn a phrase, especially when

it came to imagery and metaphor. Begrudging compliment paid, the condemnation resumed: Thoreau played at rugged self-sufficiency while squatting on borrowed land, in a house built with a borrowed axe.

There is one charge omitted by the indictment's otherwise thorough author—James Russell Lowell, writing in the *Atlantic Monthly* in 1865, when Thoreau's grave was still fresh. Lowell neglected to mention everyone's favorite incriminating biographical factoid about Thoreau: that during the two years he spent at Walden Pond, his mother sometimes did his laundry.

"There is one writer in all literature whose laundry arrangements have been excoriated again and again, and it is not Virginia Woolf, who almost certainly never did her own washing, or James Baldwin, or the rest of the global pantheon," the essayist Rebecca Solnit observed not long ago. "Only Henry David Thoreau has been tried in the popular imagination and found wanting for his cleaning arrangements."

Recently, as if to celebrate the sesquicentennial of Lowell's indictment, a new one appeared in *The New Yorker* under a funny title, "Pond Scum." Its author is Kathryn Schulz, a science writer, essayist, and environmental journalist—among our generation's best. Perhaps because science writers and environmental journalists are expected to revere Thoreau, and perhaps because many actually do, Schulz presents her new indictment as a heresy, one that aims to deliver a bracing corrective to the prevailing and puffed-up opinion of America's original nature boy.

On Twitter she joked that she'd need to go into witness protection, that's how heretical her heresy was. When the vendetta of Thoreau fans failed to materialize the way *Gatsby* fans had in response to a previous essay she'd written, she tweeted: "In a rumble between the rabid *Gatsby* fans and the rabid *Walden* fans, the *Gatsby* fans would win. (More of them, and sharper knives.)" On my Twitter stream, you'd think rabid *Walden* fans would be somewhat more populous than on Twitter's high seas. I've quarreled with Thoreau in print—and far more often, in my head—but I've also mined his prose for epigraphs, and I'll confess, shamefully, that I once tweeted a line of his— "Princess Adelaide has the whooping cough. #thoreau #meta-tweet"—that no one retweeted or favorited (sad emoji).* But to my surprise, even on my Twitter stream, the responses to Schulz's axe job were mostly gleeful.

"This is the Thoreau takedown I have been waiting for my entire life. Thank you," tweeted one of my favorite twitterers. "First, they came for Atticus Finch. Now, Thoreau? Brilliant," tweeted another. To which I initially responded with quiet desperation, while listening to a different drummer in the distance. I am far from jesting (wink emoji).

I can think of a few explanations for the failure of Thoreau fans to materialize, armed with flutes and truly excellent pencils instead of daggers and shivs, but the explanation I find most plausible is this: Schulz's heresy turns out to be more orthodox than she thought.

---

* The passage in which that line appears: "We are in great haste to construct a magnetic telegraph from Maine to Texas; but Maine and Texas, it may be, have nothing important to communicate.... As if the main object were to talk fast and not to talk sensibly. We are eager to tunnel under the Atlantic and bring the Old World some weeks nearer to the New; but perchance the first news that will leak through into the broad, flapping American ear will be that the Princess Adelaide has the whooping cough."

It's true, few people actually bother to read Thoreau anymore. And Schulz is right that those who revere him without reading him, preferring to sample him aphoristically on inspirational posters, have simplified both him and his work beyond recognition. But Schulz does the same, replacing the distortions of hagiography with those of caricature, and the caricature has been drawn before, by James Russell Lowell and many others since.

Here, several years ago, is Jill Lepore, also writing in *The New Yorker*: "one senses that [Thoreau] preferred jail to a cabin crowded with visitors." He "loved his solitude (a friend of his once said that he 'imitates porcupines successfully'), and he hated hearing news. . . . Above all, he cherished his manly self-sufficiency (even though he carried his dirty laundry to Concord for his mother to wash)."

Here's Bill Bryson, reassuring the readers of *A Walk in the Woods* that despite his own concerns about the environmental degradation to be witnessed along the Appalachian Trail, he's no Thoreau, whom he dismisses as "inestimably priggish and tiresome."

Here's Garrison Keillor in a syndicated column, presenting to the above-average children of Lake Wobegon a comforting portrait of the below-average hermit of Walden Pond:

> A sorehead and loner whose clunky line about marching to your own drummer has found its way into a million graduation speeches. Thoreau tried to make a virtue out of lack of rhythm. He said that the mass of men lead lives of quiet desperation. Okay, but how did he know? He didn't talk to that many people. He wrote elegantly about independence and forgot to thank his mom for doing his laundry.

The caricature has been drawn so many times and so redundantly that Robert Sullivan spent an entire book, published in 2009, trying to excavate Thoreau from beneath the encrustations of both unflattering and beatifying hearsay. *The Thoreau You Don't Know*, Sullivan's book is called. I recommend it, though Sullivan's effort, like Solnit's, seems to have been a futile one.

For now here comes Schulz, touching up the old cartoon. She doesn't mention Thoreau's mother doing the laundry, perhaps because she doesn't have to. She gives us her cookie-baking instead. "The real Thoreau," she writes, as if channeling Lowell, "was in the fullest sense of the word, self-obsessed: narcissistic, fanatical about self-control, adamant that he required nothing beyond himself to understand and thrive in the world." He was a hypocrite, and *Walden* a sham piece of "cabin porn," since he wasn't really roughing it—not like Laura Ingalls Wilder's Ma and Pa, homesteading and churchgoing on territory recently vacated by the heathens, building a little house on a stolen prairie. (My immigrant ancestors did the same.)

So far as frontier literature goes, at least for grown-ups, I'd take Cather over Wilder, but the more salient point is that Thoreau knew full well the difference between a suburban woodlot and the wilderness. In *The Maine Woods*, after returning to Concord from a trek to Mount Katahdin, he expresses his preference for "partially cultivated country." At Walden and in *Walden*, he *was* playing at roughing it, Schulz is right about that, and playing at much else too—farming and bookkeeping, for instance. Right there, in *Walden*'s opening paragraph, he locates the pond *in* the town, and a few paragraphs down says he's traveled widely in Concord—which is a kind of joke.

Thoreau's contemporaries didn't like him, Schulz tells us, relying presumably on the testimony of one of his Harvard classmates, John Weiss, who went on to become a minister and a writer who would likely be mostly forgotten now were it not for his portrait of his former classmate, with whom he was only casually acquainted. Weiss defended Thoreau's unorthodox religious views from critics, but he also made much of Thoreau's cold demeanor and clammy hands; also, his ugly, big-nosed physiognomy. (It's true, Thoreau was a homely man, and knew it.) In her essay on Thoreau's laundry, Solnit quotes a firsthand impression of Thoreau, written by the abolitionist Daniel Conway after Thoreau and his sister broke the law by sheltering a fugitive slave. Conway's character sketch bears repeating far more than do the collegiate memories of a classmate Thoreau hardly knew:

> In the morning I found the Thoreaus agitated by the arrival of a colored fugitive from Virginia, who had come to their door at daybreak. Thoreau took me to a room where his excellent sister, Sophia, was ministering to the fugitive. . . . I observed the tender and lowly devotion of Thoreau to the African. He now and then drew near to the trembling man, and with a cheerful voice bade him feel at home, and have no fear that any power should again wrong him. The whole day he mounted guard over the fugitive, for it was a slave-hunting time. But the guard had no weapon, and probably there was no such thing in the house. The next day the fugitive was got to Canada, and I enjoyed my first walk with Thoreau.

How to reconcile Conway's firsthand Thoreau with Schulz's secondhand one?

Like Lowell, she presents the sales figures of Thoreau's books, published "to middling critical and popular acclaim," as a measure of their value and of their unlikable author. Let the record show: Whitman, whom Schulz compares favorably to Thoreau, fared worse, for whatever that's worth—not much, I'd say. The initial print run of *Leaves of Grass* sold just 795 copies to *Walden*'s 2,000. Both books have made up for it since.

Of the many charges her indictment levels against Thoreau, the one Schulz gives greatest weight is the charge of Puritanical misanthropy. "Food, drink, friends, family, community, tradition, most work, most education, most conversation: all this he dismissed as outside the real business of living," she writes. Biographically, she is mistaken on nearly every count.

"One misperception that has persisted is that he was a hermit who cared little for others," says Elizabeth Witherell, who has spent a few decades editing a critical edition of Thoreau's collected works. "He was active in circulating petitions for neighbors in need. He was attentive to what was going on in the community. He was involved in the Underground Railroad." He quit his first teaching job, in protest, because he was expected to administer corporal punishment, and struggled to find a new one. He cared about education so much that he and his brother started their own school, the curriculum for which combined book study and field work. Along with rhetoric, Latin, and math, the Thoreau brothers offered a course on natural philosophy—what we would now call ecology—for which they took their students on field trips and sampling expeditions into the surrounding woods. He loved watermelons, and threw an annual watermelon party for his friends, of whom he had plenty. Children were especially fond of him. Sophia and Thoreau's mother were founding members of the Concord Female Anti-Slavery Society, and Thoreau invited them to convene at least one meeting that we know of at his cabin in the woods, to celebrate the anniversary of the emancipation of slaves in the Indies. As for family, he lived most of his life in his parents' boarding house, paying rent and helping out as a handyman. He was very handy. He could dance, and play music. He wrote lovingly about his father, mother, and siblings in his journals, and they wrote lovingly about him, and he was so devastated by his brother's death that he developed symptoms of tetanus in sympathy.

Schulz mentions Thoreau's visits home, and the visits he received, but accuses him of downplaying them in *Walden* while overlooking the chapter devoted to that subject, "Visitors," which includes this famous passage: "I had three chairs in my house; one for solitude, two for friendship, three for society. When visitors came in larger and unexpected numbers there was but the third chair for them all, but they generally economized the room by standing up. It is surprising how many great men and women a small house will contain. I have had twenty-five or thirty souls, with their bodies, at once under my roof, and yet we often parted without being aware that we had come very near to one another."

Schulz describes Thoreau as "well off." His biographer, Walter Harding, says the Thoreaus often lived in poverty. Who's right? Perhaps both, depending what you mean by "poverty" and "well off." In Thoreau's later years, after the family pencil business succeeded, with his help, they secured a place in

Concord's middle class, but for most of Thoreau's short, tubercular life, they were financially insecure. The portrait he draws in the opening paragraphs of *Walden* of a poor laboring man reduced to mindless, mechanical toil while pursued by creditors bears some resemblance to his own father, a failed grocer who supposedly sold his wedding ring to pay his debts while neglecting to collect those of his customers. The family turned their home into a boarding house to supplement his income.

At Harvard, which back then was a professional school for ministers, lawyers, and teachers, Thoreau interrupted his studies periodically to earn his tuition. The seeds of *Walden* were sown in the wake of the Panic of 1837, during a period of financial turmoil and rising inequality, when New England's agrarian economy was vanishing, giving way to industrialism. Sullivan tells us that shortly before the panic struck, 63 percent of Concord's citizens owned no land, and "about fifty men"— in a town of 2,000—controlled half the wealth. The freedoms promised by the Revolution seemed increasingly jeopardized by the marketplace. In the textile mills, the mass of men—and women—did indeed lead lives of quiet desperation, as Thoreau would have known. His friend Orestes Brownson was one of America's first labor agitators. Even college graduates had a hard time finding work. There's a reason Thoreau addresses *Walden* to "poor students."

How to live in America with the intellectual freedom of a Montaigne but without Montaigne's rank and wealth? How to study the cosmos with the ardor and insight of a Humboldt but without a boat ticket or a patron? The answers were, for a poor student, no more obvious then than they are now, especially if you happened to be a poor student whose conscience was troubled by your country's dependence on slave labor in the South and on industrial exploitation in the North. What was a poor student to do? Go West?

That was one option, availed by many, among them Laura's Pa. And if you objected to the imperialistic land grab in the West? What then was a poor student to do? Despair? Quietly? Suck it up? While minding your own business? Thoreau's advice to poor students is not so different from Grace Paley's: "If you want to write, keep a low overhead."

Like many caricaturists before her, Schulz doesn't distinguish much between the work and the man, but the "I" of *Walden* is a persona, one that Thoreau adopts for reasons more rhetorical than autobiographical. His "I" is in many ways akin to the speaker in a Dickinson poem, and like Dickinson, who'd read and admired him, he tends to write in riddling metaphors. He thought of *Walden* as a poem, in the Greek sense of that word, not nonfiction, a genre and label that did not then exist. Solnit aptly describes Thoreau's cabin as "a laboratory for a prankish investigation of work, money, time, and space by our nation's or empire's trickster-in-chief." It's almost always a bad idea to take him too literally, as Schulz repeatedly does. "Thoreau regarded humor as he regarded salt, and did without," Schulz informs us—a good line, if it were true.

In *Walden*, Thoreau provides two of his favorite recipes—for "green sweet-corn boiled with salt" and bread made from "Indian meal and salt." He relished the seasoning of humor even more. In many of *Walden*'s most outlandish or seemingly ridiculous passages, Thoreau was kidding, employing hyperbole and metaphor and wordplay for satirical and, yes, humorous effect. Some of his contemporaries, at least, got the jokes.

Before it appeared as the first chapter of *Walden*, Thoreau delivered "Economy"—"dry, sententious, condescending," too long, is how Schulz describes it—as a well-attended lecture at the Concord Lyceum. According to a review that appeared in the *Salem Observer*, the lecture created "quite a sensation." It "was done in an admirable manner, in a strain of exquisite humor, with a strong undercurrent of delicate satire against the follies of the times." It kept the audience, the reviewer notes, "in almost constant mirth." After attending one of Thoreau's lectures, Emerson recorded in his journal, perhaps enviously, "They laughed till they cried."

Where are the jokes? In plain sight. Schulz even quotes some of them, for instance in this passage, on his objection to doormats: "As I had no room to spare within the house, nor time to spare within or without to shake it, I declined it, preferring to wipe my feet on the sod before my door. It is best to avoid the beginnings of evil." That last sentence is a parody of a Puritanical sermon, not a sincere emulation of one, just as Thoreau's fastidious bookkeeping is a satirical parody of business. Throughout *Walden* but especially in "Economy," Thoreau is mocking the usual sources of Yankee common sense—newspapers, sermons, but especially the language of commerce—irreverently turning the platitudes and the clichés inside out and upside down.

He even indulges in a little bathroom humor. He makes fart jokes about beans. Describing his long walks, he writes, "I have watered the red huckleberry, the sand cherry and the nettle

tree, the red pine and the black ash, the white grape and the yellow violet, which might have withered else in dry seasons." Is
this Thoreau piously boasting that he walks around like some
American St. Francis with a watering can tending the tender
sprigs? No, it's him with a satirical mask on saying that he
walks around pissing—charitably, virtuously, industriously—
on trees and bushes. Without letting the satirical mask slip,
he expresses mock surprise that, despite his sincere effort to
"mind [his] business," his business being pissing on bushes and
trees, his townsmen "would not after all admit me into the list
of town officers, nor make my place a sinecure with a moderate
allowance." He is, in the Shakespearean sense, playing the fool.

Perhaps the most curiously contrary charge Schulz levels
against Thoreau is *incuriosity*. Provincial, yes—in his travels. In
his reading, he was cosmopolitan. But *incurious*? The man was
endlessly investigating phenomena both natural and human.
On his provincial travels in Concord but also to Cape Cod and
Maine, he was endlessly interviewing strangers—lumberjacks,
oystermen, farmers. He romanticized Native Americans as
noble savages, and exoticized them, representing the broken
English of those he met phonetically in ways that now make
us cringe, but unlike most of his contemporaries, he also made
a point of meeting them, interviewing them, traveling with
them, and he tried to learn of and from them on his long walks.

His data set from Walden pond is still consulted by climate
scientists. On his field trips, he collected flora and fauna for the
Swiss-born Harvard biologist Louis Agassiz, and the botanical
archives of the Harvard University Herbaria presently contain
some 1,100 different plant specimens originally botanized by
Thoreau. My own favorite biographical vignette about Thoreau

is this one, from an essay by Guy Davenport: The Thoreau who befriended Agassiz, Davenport writes, "was a scientist, the pioneer ecologist, one of the few men in America with whom [Agassiz] could talk, as on an occasion when the two went exhaustively into the mating of turtles, to the dismay of their host for dinner, Emerson."

Curiosity is what drew Thoreau to the shipwreck he writes about in *Cape Cod*, Exhibit A in Schulz's indictment. Death was yet another phenomenon he sought to understand by studying it up close. Quoting one passage out of the many paragraphs Thoreau devotes to the seaside carnage he witnessed, Schulz pegs him as a heartless bastard, a sort of Transcendental sociopath, indifferent to suffering. "On the whole," that passage begins, "it was not so impressive a scene as I might have expected. If I had found one body cast upon the beach in some lonely place, it would have affected me more." He's describing here a paradox that we've all surely experienced: When the sufferings of strangers multiply, they have a way of growing abstract in our imaginations, as do the feelings they elicit, hence the numbed indifference casualty statistics can induce, whereas the suffering of a single individual can move us easily to outrage or tears. We saw this paradox illustrated not long ago by a photo of another drowned refugee who died seeking sanctuary, Syrian rather than Irish this time, a three-year-old, Aylan Kurdi, whose corpse washed up on the Greek island of Kos rather than on Cape Cod.

To turn her one incriminating passage into evidence of Thoreau's misanthropy, moreover, Schulz has to ignore the rest of the chapter, originally published as an essay in *Putnam's*

Magazine. It is a kind of extended prose elegy, written to bear witness to and make sense of the tragedy that befell that shipload of Irish immigrants. Upon arriving at the beach, Thoreau memorializes the dead, and individualizes them, and makes us see them in prose as graphic, almost, as a photograph but more eloquent:

> I saw many marble feet and matted heads as the cloths were raised, and one livid, swollen, and mangled body of a drowned girl,—who probably had intended to go out to service in some American family,—to which some rags still adhered, with a string, half concealed by the flesh, about its swollen neck; the coiled-up wreck of a human hulk, gashed by the rocks or fishes, so that the bone and muscle were exposed, but quite bloodless,—merely red and white,—with wide-open and staring eyes, yet lustreless, dead-lights; or like the cabin windows of a stranded vessel, filled with sand.

The essay is almost the inverse of what Schulz takes it for: not a symptom of cold indifference, an antidote to it. The stoicism of the passage she quotes is also explained by what follows it, a homily on the consolations of the afterlife. "All their plans and hopes burst like a bubble! Infants by the score dashed on the rocks by the enraged Atlantic Ocean!" Thoreau exclaims, and then reassures his readers and, one senses, himself that the souls of the drowned have reached the safe harbor of heaven— this at a time when many New England Protestants regarded Irish Catholic immigrants as Papist infidels whose arrival in famine ships posed a threat to American democracy.

It's at such devotional moments that my own objections to

Thoreau tend to arise. When he goes sauntering to the holy land, I have trouble following him there. For all his irreverence toward the church, for all his open-minded, influence-seeking study of Eastern and Western philosophy, he is a profoundly Christian writer, and one whose faith is, on the page at least, less conflicted than Dickinson's or Melville's.

It's not, as Schulz asserts, that Thoreau wished to retreat to some prelapsarian Eden. The Transcendentalist heresy was to reject the doctrine of the Fall entirely. We are not innately fallen, and Eden is all around us, Thoreau and Emerson believed. You didn't have to seek divinity in a church. You could find it anywhere—in the mating habits of turtles, at the scene of a shipwreck, in pond scum—if you knew how to look and listen, and at looking and listening Thoreau, the apprentice, surpassed his master. "The morning wind forever blows, the poem of creation is uninterrupted; but few are the ears that hear it," Thoreau writes in *Walden*, paraphrasing Christ. I do not believe in intelligent design, or—on most days—that divinity infuses the cosmos, and yet Thoreau's artful efforts at revelation in *Walden* do have the power to make both time and place seem numinous, which is its own consolation. He influenced Proust and Marilynne Robinson as well as Gandhi, after all.

Schulz rightly notes that Thoreau's theology underpins the political philosophy he articulates in "Resistance to Civil Government" (now commonly known as "Civil Disobedience"). Like Gandhi, Martin Luther King, and yes, Kim Davis, he believed in higher laws deriving from a higher power, which does make his political philosophy—and Gandhi's, and MLK's—problematic for those of us who don't. And Schulz is right, too, that in that essay's provocative opening paragraphs, though less so as he goes on, Thoreau can sound like a utopian anarcholibertarian. But to twist his protest against the crime of slavery and the illegal invasion of Mexico into the actions of an egotistical forerunner of the godless Ayn Rand, a forerunner who also nonetheless suffers from a god complex and an antipathy to Industry, is a feat of contortionism as well as contrarianism.

A few paragraphs in, Thoreau clarifies his position. It's not "no government" that he wants but "a better government," which is reasonable enough, considering the shortcomings he identifies. "Unjust laws exist: shall we be content to obey them," he asks, "or shall we endeavor to amend them, and obey them until we have succeeded, or shall we transgress them at once?" That is a genuinely difficult moral question, one that is with us still. Recall that those unjust laws then included the Constitution's Fugitive Slave Law, soon to be strengthened by the 1850 Fugitive Slave Act, the prohibitions of which were being fiercely debated when Thoreau went to jail. Every participant in the Underground Railroad chose transgression over obedience. What would Schulz have had them do? Obey?

Recall, too, that people went to prison to attain the rights Kim Davis considers sacrilegious. That Davis also chose transgression does not absolve us from confronting such choices ourselves, and neither should it spare Davis from the consequences of hers. The government to which she's beholden should not let her abuse the powers of her office; that would only exemplify the sort of abuse that worried Thoreau. Let the marriages proceed. But let her go to prison and share her opinions with those who care to listen. Transgression, for Thoreau, is not the end in itself. The opposite. It is, he argues, a "beginning." And it is, Schulz's assertion to the contrary notwithstanding, a deeply democratic gesture. Quoth: "Cast your whole vote, not a strip of paper merely, but your whole influence. A minority is powerless while it conforms to the majority; it is not even a minority then; but it is irresistible when it clogs by its whole weight." The purpose of civil disobedience as of "Civil Disobedience" is to persuade; to shift the needle on the nation's moral compass, and in the case of gay marriage the needle is moving swiftly away from Davis, not toward her.

As I'm writing this, the writer and climate activist Bill McKibben is getting himself arrested at an Exxon station. And now I'm thinking, *Why am I not doing the same?* And now I'm thinking, *I'm the one in need of an apologist, not Thoreau.* Which is what civil disobedience can do: disturb those of us who assent, but silently, and rouse us from our quiescence. Thoreau doesn't "intuit" his reasons for transgressing, as Schulz asserts, or simply dial up his private line to God. Yes, he believes the angels are on the side of the abolitionist cause, justice too, and history, but he also builds the case, subjecting his own thinking to "logical scrutiny," laying his reasoning out.

Nor is it at all fair to say, as Schulz does, that "Thoreau never understood that life itself is not consistent—that what worked for a well-off Harvard-educated man without dependents or obligations might not make an ideal universal code." In "Resistance to Civil Government," he underscores and wrestles with precisely that difference. A number of his abolitionist neighbors, he writes, are afraid to transgress for fear of "the consequences to their property and family." He sympathizes with them so fully he imagines himself in their place: "[I]f I deny the authority of the State when it presents its tax bill, it will soon take and waste all my property, and so harass me and my children without end. This is hard." Yes, it is, and Thoreau does not shy from the difficulty.

And he himself is difficult. To my mind the better question to ask about Thoreau isn't why we love him, because most of us don't. Most of us ignore him, and a large number of those who pay him any mind seem to loathe him or find him ridiculous. At the high school where I once taught American literature, *Walden* is no longer on the syllabus, and although the sample size is unscientific, as best I can recall, few of the adolescent New Yorkers I forced *Walden* on cottoned to it. The better question, or at least the harder one for me, is why it is that ever since his untimely death in 1862 we've been having this same argument. Saint or fraud, idol or arrogant prick: Why do we seem to need him to be one or the other?

He was flawed, full of contradictions, and in *Walden* endeavored to document the changing seasons of his thoughts and moods as painstakingly as he did the depths and temperatures of Walden. So he liked trains, and also didn't. My feelings about air travel and smart phones are similarly conflicted. He was of his time, and of his place, and worked hard to attain a vantage from which he could perceive both. "*Who* are we? *where* are we?" he once asked because for him those questions were both excellent and inseparable. He sometimes sounds like a libertarian, sometimes like a progressive, sometimes like a conservative, conflicted as he was about tradition and change. He wrote so much and so contradictorily—he was an essayist, in other words—you could probably cherry-pick a quote to recommend him for membership in the John Birch Society, the

Communist Party, the Chamber of Commerce, or the Weather Underground if you wanted to. He had old-fashioned, stoical ideas about manliness and prized it a bit overmuch, but he also considered Margaret Fuller a soul mate.

And he was a poor student who once lost a hound, a bay horse, and a turtle dove and spent his whole life searching for them; a moral philosopher; a patriot and a dissident; a prose stylist so exquisite Dickinson, Frost, Tolstoy, Proust, Carson, Robinson, Dillard, and Schulz admired his sentences; who tried his best to live and write deliberately, and succeeded better than most; an epic perambulist and a committed abolitionist; a sufferer of tuberculosis from his youth to his death who nevertheless ascended Mount Katahdin; a naturalist who studied a pond, scum and all, so curiously and attentively he glimpsed an ecosystem and perhaps even a cosmos through the distorted mirror of his own reflection. "I am not worth seeing personally—the stuttering, blundering, clod-hopper that I am," Thoreau, the indicted egotist, once wrote. Why can't we take him at his word?

FALLING

How womankind, more than men, stand it I do not know;
but I have ground to suspect that most of them do not
stand it at all.

—*Henry David Thoreau, "Walking"*

Ascension

Seeking relief from my father's long commute and my mother's discontent, we moved to Mount Davidson from the
suburban lowlands of South San Francisco in 1976, the year the
cross fell dark. Named for geographer and nature lover George
Davidson, a charter member of the Sierra Club, this tallest of
San Francisco's hills pleased my brother and me inordinately
for the simple narcissistic reason that our father's name was
David and we were his sons. Our mountain, for that's how we
thought of it, was a landscape of contradiction, a wilderness in
the midst of a metropolis, on one side of which wildflowers,
poison oak, and tall grasses flourished, while on the other a
forest of blue-gum eucalyptus trees, transplanted in the 1880s
by a mining millionaire, creaked like ship masts in the fog. A
public park owned by a secular government, in the depths of

the Great Depression the peak had become home to the largest cross on Earth, a 103-foot-tall monstrosity of concrete and
steel. Some 50,000 San Franciscans had gathered for the dedication ceremony, held March 24, 1934, at the summit. Far away
in Washington, D.C., at precisely 7:30 P.M. Pacific Standard
Time, President Roosevelt depressed the golden key of his
executive telegraph, an electric signal leapt the continent, and
atop Mount Davidson the cross, lit from below by twelve 1,000-
watt lamps, blazed into the night sky like a flaming sword. It
would continue to glow, a lunar effigy on the San Francisco
skyline, off and on for the next forty-two years, until 1976,
when—except for a few days at Christmas and Easter—the
national energy crisis extinguished it.

The year before we moved to the mountain, when I was
almost three and my brother was five, our mother had run away.
For nine months—or was it eight? or six? testimonies conflict,
as they always do; memories fail, as they always do; the record
as always is unclear—she'd lived by herself in a boarding hotel
near the train yards of South San Francisco. The first night
she was gone I woke up, terrified that something horrible had
befallen us. Above me, the mattress of my brother's bunk had
begun to shed its gauzy underside, which hung down in strings
that I liked to pluck at, making them longer. Atop the dresser
our fish tank gurgled and glowed. A year later, on the morning we moved to Mount Davidson, I would try to carry it still
full of water out to the truck and succeed only in dunking the
lid far enough for the bulb inside to electrify the tank's lonely
resident, a zebra fish, which on the night my mother left drifted
obliviously through plastic kelp, a rebuke to the hysteria that
had awakened me. Uncharacteristically brave in the darkness,

I conducted a thorough investigation of the premises. In the bedroom, where my mother usually could be found, my giant father, snoring and alone, sprawled diagonally atop the tangled sheets, as if dropped there from a great height. I looked in closets, under furniture, even inside the dishwasher (from which, I distinctly remember, steam rose).

Once every few weeks, our father drove us to visit our mother at the boarding hotel she'd fled to. I remember another night, fatherless this time, when we stayed there, drinking hot chocolate from the speckled enamel cups we normally reserved for camping trips, listening to the chatter and hiss of the switch engine moving boxcars around in the yard below. Seated across from us, our mother peeled an orange and arrayed the sections into stars upon two plates. She'd had trouble lighting the burner of the stove, and the room smelled sweetly of gas. It was Halloween. My brother was dressed as Robin Hood, and I, though smaller, was Little John. In our matching felt tunics and feathered felt caps, we went trick-or-treating up and down the dingy carpeted hallways of the hotel, knocking on the numbered doors of strangers who had not expected us. Afterward our mother tucked us into her only bed. Sitting in the dark beside us, stroking our hair, she led us in a recitation of the Lord's Prayer. I loved the sound of the old words—the incantation of trespasses and daily bread, the casting of spells, *thy kingdom come, thy will be done*—though it would be years before I understood them; before I grasped that these trespasses differed from those prohibited on fences. When we addressed "Our Father," meaning God, it was our real father I pictured: Our father of the white lab coat. Our father of the choir robe and the rosewood pipe. Our father of the brass trombone.

A few weeks after that dreamlike Halloween, as suddenly as she'd vanished and as inexplicably, our mother returned, and with the sort of unanticipated joy I would eventually learn to welcome without question, our parents began looking at new houses. Upon first visiting 475 Molimo Drive, the postwar, earthquake-proof cube of a rowhouse that I will always think of as home, our mother fell in love with it. When the fog was low, her bedroom windows gazed out 750 feet above sea level onto an ocean of clouds through which the tops of neighboring mountains—Potrero Hill, Twin Peaks, Mount Sutro with its television tower—protruded like islands in a heavenly archipelago. On clear days, you could see all the way to San Francisco Bay, where the tiny yachts on the blue water resembled cabbage butterflies on a picnic blanket. Even the gleaming skyscrapers downtown seemed diminutive, like scale models of themselves. The back windows of the house looked out onto the mountain's eastern face, the dry face, covered most of the year in a yellow pelt of rattlesnake grass, foxtail, and wild oat, except for a few weeks in early spring when California poppies lit up like orange votives among the new green shoots, and those weeks in summer when the dry grass burned, as it did most summers.

From the kitchen door, a path led out into the garden, climbed a flight of stone stairs beneath an awning of overgrown ivy, and snaked its way through terraced beds, which my father would plant with vegetables and flowers, past a pool of nasturtiums, under the oxblood leaves of a wild plum, to a garden gate, on the other side of which it continued up the mountain, ascending, finally, to the concrete steps of the 103-foot-tall cross. My father hoped this new home among the clouds would make my mother happy, and for a little while it did.

Forest Christians

Not long after we moved to the mountain, my father, then chief resident in surgery at UCSF, began coming home to chaos—his sons fighting, dinner unprepared, his wife locked in her room. Some nights she would emerge only to pull on her coat and disappear. Where she went I was never sure, though the evidence usually pointed west, to the far side of the mountain, the foggy side, invisible from our windows. In 1920, after visiting the forest that grows there, James Decatur, the Western Union official and YMCA director whose idea it had been to build the Mount Davidson cross, wrote that the "peace and quiet was so profound that it seemed almost unbelievable that the noise and roar of a great city was only a few minutes behind." Losing herself in the understory for hours at a time, my mother would return with pockets full of scavengings—mossy twigs, lichen-covered rocks, the spotted, crescent-shaped leaves and germinal buttons that showered from the branches of the blue-gum eucalyptus—which she would arrange into still lifes on our mantelpiece.

My father, raised Methodist, was a practicing Presbyterian. He chose the church because of its choir's excellence. My mother, also raised Methodist, was a convert to Catholicism. The parochial school they sent us to was Episcopalian. In truth, we belonged to all and none of these denominations. We were at heart members of a flock that I once heard called, derisively, "forest Christians"—latter-day followers of that characteristically American brand of pantheism whose founding prophets were Henry David Thoreau and John Muir.

In the Bible, wilderness is either a sanctuary to which prophets flee from the persecution of tyrants and toward the call of
God, or else it is a purgatory through which chosen people
wander, doing penance for their love of Mammon. In the scriptures of forest Christians, however, the untamed refuges of
North America are wilderness and promised land both, and
to be exiled there is not perdition but deliverance. My father's
worship of nature was more pastoral (he spent his weekends
tending his vegetable garden); my mother's, more druidic (she
favored oceans and woods). Both regarded the California wilderness as a new Eden, every wild strawberry and manzanita
bush an encryption of divinity.

Forest Christians are not to be confused with hippies, with
whom they share many political affinities but few cultural
ones. Although my mother counseled draft dodgers and demonstrated at the 1968 Democratic Convention in Chicago, neither of my parents experimented with drugs or free love. (My
mother still sometimes regrets not having become a nun, and
to this day my father claims never to have been drunk.) Fri-
day nights on Molimo Drive, during those rare weeks when my
parents were not too distracted by their disintegrating marriage, we played environmentally themed board games that
my mother had mailed away for—mind-numbingly didactic
diversions printed on recycled cardboard. Save the Whales,
one was called; Nectar Collector, another. Her favorite was
the Ungame, in which players rolled dice and moved their
tokens in pointless, hypothetically endless laps around the
board, stopping at places with names like Worry Wharf or
Fearful Forest or Cheerful Chalet. On each turn, you would
draw a card that would instruct you to reveal something about

yourself—one blessing you were grateful for, say, or a lie you'd once told. If the card asked whether you'd been unhappy today and you answered in the affirmative, you'd be banished to Happy House for a turn. The game could never be won or lost. You just stopped playing when you'd grown bored of it, which usually didn't take long. To my mother's dismay, we preferred Monopoly and Risk.

Family vacations we invariably spent out-of-doors—skiing in Yosemite, strolling among the gargantuan sequoias in Muir Woods, inspecting the obscene noses of the elephant seals at Año Nuevo State Park. One summer, we waded through subterranean pools in the caverns of the Pinnacles. Another—the last the four of us ever spent together—we backpacked to the summit of Half Dome, stopping on the way to swim naked in a lake fed by melting snow. My mother never wanted these vacations to end. Back in South San Francisco, just prior to her first desertion, she'd learned of a Quaker commune in the redwood forest near Santa Cruz and, imagining a peaceful utopia among the ferns, decided that our family should join. We'd spent a weekend there, but the place had disappointed her, as such places always would. Other times the escapes she sought were purely spiritual. She was a serial convert, periodically changing churches or gurus or even faiths, setting her Catholicism aside for a fling with Quakerism, or New Age astrology, only to return to Catholicism, her fervor mysteriously restored, and with each new enthusiasm she'd attempt to convert us too. When she proselytized, her temper, always stormy, attained hurricane force. Against her torrents of outrage, my father would pile up rhetorical sandbags—what exactly was she so upset about? what exactly did she want from him?—that angered her all the more. Over the course of a few days, her righteous gales would exhaust themselves, and the breezes of despair would waft through our house once again.

Since shortly after I was born, she'd been seeing a psychiatrist, who had prescribed a daily dose of antidepressants, but they hadn't worked, and she'd stopped taking them. One day my father came home from work on his lunch hour to fetch something he'd forgotten and found the house empty. With my brother and me in school, my mother, who'd jettisoned her nursing career in order to raise us, spent her days alone, keeping house, taking walks and naps. Her absence on this particular day was not remarkable; the note she'd left on my father's desk was. In it, she apologized for what she was about to do.

He called the police, who alerted the authorities at the Golden Gate Bridge to keep an eye out for a jumper matching my mother's description: small Caucasian female, five feet three, dark brown hair, mid-thirties. Beyond this there was little the cops could do. It was too soon to declare her missing, but they promised to page my father with any news. Next my father contacted her psychiatrist, who advised him to go settle his affairs at work and hurry home as soon as he could. He'd need to be there for the boys if she failed to show up. But by the time he returned from the hospital, she was back, behaving as if nothing out of the ordinary had happened. The note had vanished, and, at her doctor's recommendation, my father never mentioned it.

When he first told me this story, in 1994, the summer after I graduated from college, I found it hard to believe and wondered if my father could have unknowingly fabricated the incident, which my mother insists never happened. Memory, after all, is a kind of dream, and even the most dispassionate divorcé is incapable of narrating reliably scenes from a failed marriage. How could he have returned to the hospital, I asked him, when for all he knew his wife was killing herself? And afterward, how could he not have mentioned the note? Didn't he want to know where she had gone? What she'd intended to do? And why? Wasn't he terrified that someday not long thereafter she might try to go through with it? How could something like a suicide note remain secret between them?

We were sitting on a teak bench far away from Mount David-son, in another city, another state, another time zone, another latitude, on the patio of another house, where my father lived with other children and another wife. At the fringes of the porch light, where the dark began, cockroaches the size and color of candied dates scuttled through puddles on the paved walk. A rusting swing set glimmered on the lawn. It had rained earlier that day, a big tropical rain, and the night was raucous with the elation of toads. As he considered my questions, massaging the bridge of his nose and dangling his glasses by one arm, my father seemed to be attempting to decipher this amphibian chorale, which perhaps contained urgent news.

Yes, of course he'd been terrified, he said finally, but look-ing back on it, he had no idea why she'd done what she'd done, or why he'd done what he'd done, any of it. Nothing about his marriage had made much sense to him then.

By 1994 my mother, too, had left San Francisco. Her money had run out, and she could no longer afford the rent. After an interlude in the Hudson Valley working for room and board at a rest home founded on the pseudomystical teachings of Rudolf Steiner, she'd washed out and up in Champaign, Illinois, where she'd stayed briefly with her parents. When they refused to let her turn their house into a Waldorf school, she'd taken a room in a place called the Thrift-O-Tel out by 1–74, and I visited her there after commencement, on my way home to my father's house from college.

We grilled kebabs beside a swimming pool no one was swimming in, and she told me things I did not wish to hear. Her stories were filled with internal contradictions and factual inaccuracies, and I did not know what to believe. She seemed to me an even less reliable narrator than my father. The more she spoke, the more sick I felt, dizzy with narrative vertigo. Then she told me the story of how she'd ridden a three-speed across America hoping to find God, herself, and a Korean boy named Dongho Kim.

Red Cross

In the summer of 1955, or else centuries ago, during one of her previous lifetimes, my mother fell in love. She'd been a Mongolian warrior once, she informed me when I was a teenager, a claim that I liked to repeat sardonically for the amusement of friends, but in the summer of 1955, she was a thirteen-year-old American girl stationed along with the rest of her family on a military base in Okinawa, Japan. The daughter of a prematurely white-haired, devoutly Methodist housewife and a violently temperamental air force colonel who'd flown bombing missions in World War II, my mother had after much pleading obtained precious permission to spend a week at a nearby Junior Red Cross Training Camp. It was the first time she'd enjoyed such independence.

The nationalities of the trainees were mixed—forty Americans, forty Japanese, and ten Koreans. My mother felt "naturally drawn" to this last group, an affinity that seems logical enough in light of her parents' infatuation with the divided peninsula. Her father had served in the Korean War, and afterward he and his wife had adopted two Korean war orphans—silent Jimmy (today a born-again Christian in North Carolina) and Helen (now married to an outdoorsman in Louisiana). During the week she spent learning to tie tourniquets and administer CPR, my mother and an older boy named Dongho Kim, also a war orphan, had formed what forty years later she referred to, poolside at the Thrift-O-Tel, as "a heart connection."

The autumn following this short-lived romance, my grandfather, a jazz trumpeter as well as a bomber pilot, retired from the military and took a civilian job teaching music at the University of Illinois, the same university, it so happened, where my paternal grandfather taught math. I had heard this part of the story many times before: how my mother's family had moved down the block from my father's; how in his senior year she'd played the lead in *Our Town*, the dead girl with the broken heart, and he'd played her father; how she'd been his date to the prom. But what I had never previously learned was that for nine years, from the age of thirteen to the day she accepted my father's proposal, my mother and Dongho Kim had maintained a prodigious, soul-searching correspondence.

Looking back on it from the vantage of the Thrift-O-Tel, with wisdom acquired during three decades in Northern California, my mother could offer only one explanation for this "deep karmic connection": She and Kim had been lovers in a previous life.

In high school, she'd dated other boys, including my father, who seemed to her like an older brother, but increasingly Dongho Kim had become "a stumbling block." She always felt bad for her dates, since she'd already given her heart to another. Finally, during her second year at a Christian women's college in Milwaukee, shaken by a heretical physics teacher who'd made her write a proof for the existence of God, my mother decided she'd waited long enough. It was time to see whether this courtship-by-correspondence was for real. And so, in the summer of 1963, twenty years old, infected with the maddening spirit of the times, driven by what she referred to now as "an internal energy," and accompanied by an irreverent art student named Pam whom she'd met the previous spring, my mother climbed aboard her three-speed and pedaled west, for California. She planned to recuperate at her grandfather's house in Santa Cruz, then work her way across the Pacific on a steamer bound for Seoul.

That afternoon, in her ferociously tidy motel room—her belongings in boxes or wrapped in plastic bags sealed with twist-ties—she read aloud to me from the travelogue she'd kept of this trip. I heard about the dangers of snakes and "flirty" boys; about flat tires and broken gears; about nights spent in laundromats, on the porches of strangers, in public parks, in a small-town jail; about a dinner with a family of fundamentalist Christians in Waterloo, Iowa, at which, when a dog had started licking her hand under the table during grace, my mother began laughing and, despite the aghast reactions of her hosts, found she was unable to stop.

In Denver, Pam the art student took a job in a candy store, and my mother crossed the Rockies by train. After biking a few days through the Utah desert alone, she'd pulled into a truck stop and hitched a ride with a teamster headed all the way to Stockton, California, from which it was a comparatively short bike trip across the San Jacinto Valley to her grandfather's front door. From start to finish, the 1,500-mile journey took her exactly forty days.

I was impressed by all this. It was more than I'd hoped to learn when I'd pulled into the parking lot at the Thrift-O-Tel; more, frankly, than I'd imagined my mother capable of. Later, I asked her for a copy of her diary, and she obliged, sending me Xeroxed pages on which she'd penciled in notations and sub-headings like those found in nineteenth-century travel narratives. "More challenges," one such annotation began, "tornado warnings, tire blow-outs, dirty restrooms." I had hoped to find in this document clues that could solve the mystery I have spent most of my life investigating, the mystery of my mother's unhappiness, and yet her diary raised as many questions as it answered. The quest it recounted seemed to me at once quixotic and heroic. On the one hand, her entries, full of adolescent ruminations on the meaning of life and anguished confessions of self-loathing, foreshadowed the desperation to come. On the other hand, her trek had been gutsy and grand, especially for a twenty-year-old girl, especially in 1963, before bra-burnings, the Equal Rights Amendment, and all the other grand, gutsy feminist endeavors I'd read about in college. Before Adrienne Rich dove into the wreck and the same year that Betty Friedan demystified the feminine, my mother had traversed the American West on a Schwinn.

The fact was, in the summer of 1994, I myself had begun to feel the machinations of an internal energy and the first tremors of uncontrollable laughter. Earlier that spring, after four years of nearly perfect grades, I'd suddenly become terrified of failure, of heights, laboring in neurotic anguish to complete an honors thesis on, of all things, the myth of the self-made man in the work of Thoreau. Unlike my mother, I trembled not to redeem God but myself. Persuaded that I needed to pay for the privileges bequeathed to me by my white male forebears, I undertook to become a feminist martyr and renounced the white male professor, a kind if politically anachronistic poet, who had been until then a spiritual father to me. In April of my senior year, driving back to school after spring break, I began weeping for no reason while crossing Indiana in a thunderstorm. I never wrote that thesis on Thoreau.

I went to the Thrift-O-Tel on a rescue mission. Equipped with my training in feminist literary theory, I hoped to make sense of my mother's vertiginous past. Throughout my adolescence, I had regarded her as a villain and an embarrassment. In college I'd come to see her as a victim, though of whom or of what I wasn't sure. In adulthood, she'd always had a room of her own. The divorce settlement generously supported her. She'd pursued several careers. After leaving my father in 1979, she'd dated several different men. And yet, liberated from marriage, from motherhood, from all obligations whatsoever, she had found not happiness but the same familiar insatiable yearning. Who was to blame? Her father? My father? Her psychiatrist? Dongho Kim? My great-grandfather, who'd converted her to Catholicism? The Judeo-Christian God? What oppressive experience could compel a woman to abandon her small children, I wondered, or lock herself for hours inside her room, or try to kill herself?

Spring's Boy

When you grow up on the slope of a mountain, altitude defines your sense of the universe as much as flatness does the lives of Nebraskans, or aridity the psychic climate of Bedouins. You acquire, for one thing, a heightened awareness of gravity. To reach our house on foot, you had to lean into the gradient and creep your way up, arduous step by arduous step, as if scaling a steep flight of stairs. Walking from the bus stop one block away, Mrs. Hickman, one of our more elderly neighbors and a smoker, paused every few yards to catch her breath. Leaving our house, on the other hand, you had to lean backward, as if preparing to do the limbo. To ascend the mountain on a bicycle was impossible, except by tacking back and forth on a ten-speed in first gear. Biking down required only a good set of brakes. You could put your feet up on the crossbar and coast for miles, hair whipping behind you, pedals spinning in the breeze. We had a term for this sort of free fall: bombing. Once, my brother and some neighbor kids affixed skate trucks to pieces of scrap lumber and held races to see which ramshackle go-cart could bomb our hill the fastest. Summers, when the wild oat and rattlesnake grass were tall and dry, we scavenged flattened produce boxes from the trash bins behind Tower Market and rode them down the mountain like sleds. After a few descents, the bulldozed grass formed a slick chute that sent us rocketing into a thicket of Scotch broom.

With our mother, whom he claimed to despise, my brother shared a taste for flight, and he sometimes enlisted me as his accomplice. One night, a few years after we moved to Mount

Davidson, we filled a backpack with canned food and ran away to the forest on the western face. Shivering among ferns, we ate cold pork and beans with plastic spoons while condensed fog and eucalyptus buttons pattered down upon us. We intended to stay the whole night, but after a few hours the darkness and the groaning trees sent us racing home, down the narrow trail, through the Scotch broom, toward the glowing windows of our house. Alone, at the kitchen table, his beloved choral music playing quietly on the hi-fi (Mozart's "Great" Mass, perhaps, or one of Bach's passions), our father wept into his handkerchief. Our mother had gone out searching. She walked all the way to Half Moon Bay and back, fifteen miles each way, arriving on our doorstep just before dawn.

At the age of twelve, two years after our parents had finally divorced, while my father and I were away at church, my brother drove off with the family car. He left behind a note saying he'd decided to move in with our widowed paternal grandmother in Illinois. Then, perched atop a pillow, his youth obscured by the visor of a Giants cap pulled low, he picked up a friend and sped south, toward the central coast. Just as he'd done when he'd found my mother's note, my father called the police, and troopers across California and Nevada began looking for a white station wagon chauffeured by a chubby twelve-year-old wearing glasses. Several hours later, broke and nearly out of gas, my brother telephoned from San Luis Obispo, and my father fetched him home. The year prior to this road trip, my brother had behaved so badly—fighting with classmates, leaping from my father's car at a stop sign on our way to school, disappearing on Saturday mornings when our mother came to take custody of us for the weekend, as the divorce agreement required—that my father, ever the doctor, had his eldest son hospitalized for psychiatric evaluation. His doctors had found nothing wrong with him besides his unhappy family, and after a few weeks of good behavior they sent him home. Nature played no part in his escapades. He wasn't running to anything; he was running away, declaring his independence not in writing but in miles. When my mother ran away, she sought something more than freedom—sanctuary, transcendence, God. And in this respect, I was more my mother's son than he was. I was her nature boy.

According to Annie Dillard, young children have no sense of wonder. "They bewilder well," she writes. "but few things surprise them. All of it is new to young children, after all, and equally gratuitous. Their parents pause at the unnecessary beauty of an ice storm coating the trees; the children look for something to throw." Maybe she's right, but whether out of genuine wonder, or simply in order to win my mother's affection, I displayed a precocious interest in the natural world. On my sixth birthday, while my guests and I were having cake at the picnic table in the back yard, a butterfly, a tiger swallowtail, had fluttered down from the mountain and alighted on my shirt, attracted perhaps by the brightly colored fabric. On legs as thin as filaments, it climbed an inch or two toward my shoulder, opened and closed its magnificent wings, and then took to the air once again. Thereafter, I became an amateur lepidopterist.

In my father's garden, there were cabbage butterflies, little white things with a single black dot on each wing (tottering over the vegetable beds they looked like thrown dice), and the occasional painted lady. But the best specimens, the tiger swallowtails and monarchs, preferred the wild anise and wild blackberry that flourished at the top of the mountain. On Saturday mornings I hiked up to chase them. Early, before the sun was high enough to burn it off, fog would settle onto the rooftops below. High above the invisible city, clutching a Skippy jar, wild yellow wings battering inside it, the gauzy sock of my dime-store net drooping over one shoulder, I imagined myself some postapocalyptic Crusoe, the sole surviving member of the human race.

Usually I practiced a catch-and-release form of lepidoptery, keeping my quarry no more than a single afternoon. During their brief captivity, I would provide them with blades of glass to perch on as well as ridiculous names gleaned from comic books—Shazam or Thor or Flash. After a few hours, I'd unscrew the perforated lid, shake these insects into the air, and watch as they wobbled homeward over the tips of the wild oat. But on one occasion, out of sadistic curiosity, I suppose, I decided not to let my prisoner go. After a few days, the creature—a gorgeous anise swallowtail with orange eyespots on its tiger-striped wings—died of unknown causes. Extracting it from the jar, I inadvertently tore off the corner of one wing, letting the colorful tatter fall to my bedroom floor, where, disembodied, it looked both magical and horrific. I nonetheless pinned my damaged specimen, once through the thorax and once through each wing, onto the corkboard above my desk and affixed a name tag just above his antennae: THUNDERBALL, it read. Eventually the pins tore through what remained of Thunderball's wings and I had to throw him away.

In addition to butterflies, I collected rocks, seashells, and arcane facts with which to impress adults. I knew, for instance, that the Greek word for "butterfly," *psyche*, also meant "soul," and that in Mexico there was a colony of spiders that lived in a web some six miles long. I knew that dolphins could swim at a top speed of forty knots, and that they sometimes killed sharks by ramming them with their noses. I knew that there were volcanic chimneys at the bottom of the ocean around which sprouted white tubeworms that could live for three centuries. I knew that horses had evolved from dog-sized animals with cloven hoofs; whales, from land mammals related distantly to bears.

The California Academy of Sciences, the natural history museum in Golden Gate Park, was for me a kind of shrine. There, rapt before the fish tanks and dioramas that illuminated the walls, I studied the clown fish and dik-diks and split geodes the way illiterate peasants used to read the scriptures in stained glass.

On trips to the shore, I waded through tidal pools, where anemones soft as internal organs sprouted from the mollusk-encrusted rocks. On the beach, when the waves receded and the sand began to simmer, I dug furiously at the bubbles, apprehending hermit crabs before they tunneled to safety. At night I made collages out of photographs clipped from juvenile nature magazines like *Ranger Rick* or *World*. One of my favorite children's books was *Wild Jeff,* a story told in black-and-white photographs of its title character gamboling about a deserted island in his swimming trunks. His parents never made an appearance, nor did any other member of the human race. This fantasy was one my brother and I shared, though, unlike me or Wild Jeff, he showed little interest in the flora and fauna of tidal pools. Parentlessness interested him greatly, motherlessness especially, nudibranchs not so much.

One afternoon when I was six, he and my mother had a fight that turned into a brawl which moved tornado-like from room to room, escalating from curses to blows. While she wrestled him into a half nelson and he pummeled her with his free arm, tears streamed down both their faces, contorted by anger into grotesque masks. Unnoticed, I slipped out the back door, hiked up the mountain, lay down in the grass, and, eyes closed, arms crossed over my chest in the customary manner of the dead, began to roll. The tall stalks, brittle with drought, crackled flat beneath me. Prickly burrs and the sticky, flame-shaped germ of the wild oat accumulated in my shoelaces and in the striped necks of my socks. At the bottom of the hill, dazed and dizzy on my back, staring through the Scotch broom at the racing clouds, I could feel my consciousness precipitating back out. Here I was—still me, still here. Staggering to my feet, I brushed off the twigs of broken grass, hiked back up, and tumbled down again. Then again, over and over, until the sun was so low even blades of grass cast long shadows and the shadow of the mountain had crept out over the city below. Maybe if the trip had lasted longer, if the slope were Himalayan in altitude, if I could have rolled for as long as Alice falls on her way to Wonderland, it might have been enough, but no matter how many times I tumbled, I never quite attained the oblivion, the bewilderment, I craved—*bewilderment,* meaning a state of wild perplexion brought on by, or analogous to, getting lost in the woods.

That night, after I'd taken one last tumble through the grass and descended the hill to our back porch, my mother, aglow with fierce calm, greeted me at the door. She crouched down and plucked the burrs and seeds from my shoelaces, collecting them in the palm of her hand as if they were offerings I'd brought for her, scolding me all the while for having left without her permission.

I have in my possession a recording she made of me around this time, on which my small child's voice can be heard stuttering through a collection of sentimental poems called *Spring's Boy*, written, my mother's voice announces at the beginning of the cassette, by a colleague of my father. When my mother sent me this tape a few years ago, I played it repeatedly, listening for clues. You can tell that the child is doing his best to impress. He reads dramatically, with exaggerated intonation and little understanding. "My mind records the color splash of woodland flowers," he brightly declares, placing the accent in "records" on the first syllable. One poem in particular, "Those Who Wait," my mother must have cherished. This is how it begins:

I weep for those who wait,
Struggling through their day-years,
their lives in saving account
and their dreams melting away.

Despite the poem's sappiness, its Romantic message is powerful and venerable, the message of countless television commercials, Hollywood films, and needlepoint wall hangings. It is also a central theme of nearly everything Thoreau wrote, though the author of *Walden* and "Civil Disobedience" almost always leavens his righteousness with a dash of irony. Like the biblical prophets, he means to antagonize his audience out of the slumber of complacency.

"I think that I cannot preserve my health and spirits," Thoreau writes in "Walking," unless I spend four hours a day at least—and it is commonly more than that—sauntering through the woods and over the hills and fields, absolutely free from all worldly engagements. . . . When sometimes I am reminded that the mechanics and shopkeepers stay in their shops not only all the forenoon, but all the afternoon too, sitting with crossed legs, so many of them—as if the legs were made to sit upon, and not to stand or walk upon—I think that they deserve some credit for not having all committed suicide long ago.

Although I recognize the condescension implicit in this stance (easy to walk out into the forenoon, if you have no obligations), these words nonetheless make me want to answer Thoreau's taunt: Oh, to break free of the entanglements of propriety and embrace a simplified life! On a few occasions I have tried answering it, impulsively quitting a depressing job or abruptly abandoning a woman I found too difficult to love. And yet, partly because of such experiments and partly because of my mother's example, I can no longer listen to Thoreau's call of the wild without hearing in it something else, something Thoreau never intended: the unmistakable melody of a siren song.

The Cross in the Mountains

If forest Christians should ever organize themselves into a proper religion, they would do well to purchase the Mount Davidson cross, which rises from a clear-cut sanctuary of dirt, and make it their St. Peter's. They missed their chance in 1997. That year, sued by litigious atheists, the City of San Francisco auctioned off the cross and the .38 acres immediately surrounding it for $26,000 to the Council of Armenian American Organizations of Northern California, which promptly rededicated it to the victims of the genocide perpetrated upon their people by the Turks.

The current monument is in fact the fifth incarnation of the Mount Davidson cross. The first, erected in 1923, was only forty feet high and made of wood. The dean of Grace Cathedral, whose parochial school my brother and I would later attend, officiated at that year's inaugural Easter sunrise service, for which the cross was illumined with searchlights. According to the *San Francisco Chronicle,* 5,000 worshipers, "boys and girls in hiking togs, Jew and Gentile, men and women in heavy wraps, Catholic and Protestant," had trudged "up the long winding pathways to the glowing cross."

Thanks to its popularity, this first cross was soon replaced with an even larger one, measuring 87 feet, which burned down the following year. In 1929, a third cross was built. Less ambitious and theoretically less flammable, this latest, 76-foot-tall version was planted in a concrete base, impastoed in stucco, and decorated with three hundred lights. Two years later, it too succumbed to flames, making way for the current 103-foot colossus. During the drought-plagued decade my family lived there, brush fires swept across Mount Davidson almost annually. Composed of 750 cubic yards of concrete and 30 tons of steel, the cross survived every one.

The practice of building shrines atop mountains long predates the crucifixion atop Golgotha. On the eve of his death, Jesus prays from the slopes of the Mount of Olives, the same spot where David, chased into the wilderness by the mutinous

Absalom, had stopped to pray nine centuries before. "The tops of mountains are among the unfinished parts of the globe," writes Thoreau, "whither it is a slight insult to the gods to climb and pry into their secrets, and try their effect on our humanity. Only daring and insolent men, perchance, go there. Simple races, as savages, do not climb mountains—their tops are sacred and mysterious tracts never visited by them." You can drive most of the way up Mount Davidson, and to climb the remaining 150 feet to its sacred and mysterious tracts requires little daring. During my childhood the numerous visitors to its top included plenty of insolent men, but also a large representation of savages.

This was, after all, California in the seventies. While my brother and I were bombing down hills on sheets of cardboard, the Symbionese Liberation Army was still robbing banks, refugees were arriving from the killing fields of Cambodia, and an evangelical psychopath named Jim Jones was still giving sermons at the People's Temple on Geary Boulevard. In November of 1978, the year I turned six, 287 children died at Jonestown. Nine days later, Dan White gunned down Mayor George Moscone and Supervisor Harvey Milk in city hall. Every Easter, multitudes of the faithful and unfaithful congregated before the Mount Davidson cross for the sunrise service held on its steps. While worshipers on picnic blankets drank coffee out of thermos cups and gospel choirs sang hymns about the Resurrection, TV camera crews collected background footage for the closing credits of the evening news.

The rest of the year, the sanctuary of dirt and trees was left largely uninhabited; the concrete stage, choirless and priest-less; the arc lights hanging amid the eucalyptus, dark; the loud-speakers, silent atop their poles. Dog walkers visited by day, revelers trespassed there at night, and after school my friends and I played at war beneath that cruciform giant, firing imaginary Gatling guns from behind its concrete trunk, which vandals were forever desecrating with graffiti. At night from our back yard you could sometimes hear motorcyclists illegally throttling their way up the fire roads for moonlit joyrides to the mountain's summit, where later, chasing butterflies with my dime-store net, I would discover the tracks their tires had inscribed in the dirt, as well as shattered bottles and condoms and campfire cinders.

On our birthdays, my mother mapped treasure hunts on the mountain, a cheap entertainment for the dozen or so friends who arrived midday bearing beribboned packages. The morning of the party, she'd wake up at dawn, a time when our dead-end street fell into a silence so profound you could hear the fog rattling the windowpanes. Imitating the quiet of the world she inhabited, she rose, dressed by the streetlight filtering through her bedroom curtains, and crept out onto our back porch, coaxing the doorknob so that the tongue of the latch slid silently into its groove. She climbed up through our terraced yard, past my father's vegetable garden, and onto the mountain, where the grass soaked her shoes with dew. For hours she surveyed the slopes and scribbled on index cards, leaving behind her a trail of clues hidden in the crotch of a branch, say, or the hollow of a stump, or at the base of the cross beneath a handful of pebbles and dirt.

On my twelfth birthday, four years after my mother had moved away for good, I created my own treasure hunt, turning the mountain into a staging ground for an elaborate Dungeons & Dragons–inspired role-playing game, wherein my party guests and I wandered among the eucalyptus trees, impersonating wizards and elves and doing battle with imaginary monsters. At the base of the cross, we made a disturbing discovery. There, arranged as neatly as graves, lay a row of pigeons, each of which had been cleanly, bloodlessly decapitated. Years later, reading Leviticus, I came across these instructions: "If your offering to the Lord is a burnt offering of birds, you shall choose your offering from turtledoves or pigeons. The priest shall bring it to the altar and wring off its head."

On several occasions rock climbers scaled the cross's sheer face, leaving behind a line of rusting pitons that ran like stitches up the back of the vertical axis. Two days before Easter, when I was eleven or twelve, I witnessed the beginning of what I'm fairly certain was the last of these attempts. Shortcutting over the mountain on my way home from school, I happened upon a crowd gathered at the foot of the cross, faces tilted toward the sky. Overhead, a dozen or so yards up, a man dangled like a spider, making his slow ascent. I didn't stick around to watch him finish. The next day I learned that in a fluke accident the climber's harness had snapped and he'd fallen to his death. At the Easter service that Sunday, the choir gathered undaunted to sing *Hallelujah!* in their purple robes. Afterward, I went looking for evidence and found, on the spot where he would have landed, a patch of gray paint no bigger than a bath towel.

My Friends Call Me Alice

In 1970, the makers of *Dirty Harry* shot that movie's dramatic showdown atop Mount Davidson, the cross serving as symbolic backdrop. Harry's nemesis in the film, a nihilistic beatnik known as the Scorpio killer who goes around sniping innocent San Franciscans for fun, is the counterculture personified, a zeitgeist-induced nightmare, Charles Manson meets merry prankster. During their big shootout, Harry takes cover behind the colossal cross, concrete chips of which explode as the bullets fly. Accompanied by atonal music, featuring long shots and close-ups of the cross that make it look ominous, the showdown is spectacular, but the scene that immediately precedes it is to my mind more memorable—memorable perhaps because it's so superfluous to the plot.

Racing up the slopes of the mountain, the lights of San Francisco spread out across the dark valleys below, Harry encounters a figure in a faded denim jacket whom he at first mistakes for the Scorpio killer but who turns out to be a baby-faced, golden-haired youth. He is a mystery, this youth. What is he doing up here in this urban wilderness, alone, at night?

"I'm Callahan," Harry says.

The kid in the denim jacket looks Harry over. Although the detective has a switchblade Scotch-taped to his ankle and the pistol with the famously long muzzle hidden in his holster, dressed in sport coat and tie, he looks as if he might teach English at a New England prep school.

"My friends call me Alice," the youth in the denim jacket says, breathless with pantomimed desire, "I *will* take a dare."

"Well, Alice, when was the last time you were busted?" says Harry.

"If you're vice," Alice says, "I'll kill myself."

"Well, do it at home."

The Sick Room

Within a few days of that afternoon I'd spent rolling through the dry grass like Wild Jeff, constellations of small bumps appeared on my skin, the telltale symptom of a brush with poison oak, which grew rampant all over the eastern face of the mountain and whose waxy, red, serrated, trifoliate leaves I had been taught from an early age to identify and avoid. I'd gotten rashes before but never one as bad as this. It erupted everywhere, spreading even to my anus and throat. My eyelids seemed to ripen into berries, swelling until it hurt to open them. I beheld the world through a fringe of eyelashes. I wore ski gloves to bed so that my body would not scratch itself in sleep. Still, I was not so miserable as one might presume. A nurse by training and a hypochondriac by nature, my mother loved us best when we were sick. It was then that we would receive the ministrations, the lavishments of affection, the reprieve from censoriousness, that she tended to withhold for fear of spoiling us. As a result, I developed a fondness for illness and injury.

At school, during gym class, if I fell during a game of dodgeball or soccer, I would lie on the ground feigning unconsciousness until my schoolmates had gathered around me, asking if I was okay. How I loved to look up at the circle of their worried faces. Sometimes my injuries were not altogether feigned. The worst athlete in my class, I attempted to compensate with heroics. I was always diving to make a tackle or catch a ball, and although rarely successful, these self-sacrificial attempts seemed to impress people. During games of cops and robbers, or of war, I loved to impersonate the dying. I could make my glasses fly from my face onto the grass as if I'd taken the butt of a rifle in the jaw, or contort spasmodically as if my body were being riddled with machine-gun fire.

I even taught myself how to hyperventilate at will, gasping and wheezing until Coach Loomis told me to "go see Mrs. Scott." Mrs. Scott was the school secretary and the closest thing we had to a nurse. She dispensed sugar cubes when your throat was sore and cups of warm saltwater to gargle when you lost a tooth. She took temperatures, applied Band-Aids, and in urgent cases made the necessary phone calls to doctors and parents. Her office adjoined the sick room, a cubicle with a cot in it where, until gym class ended, I would lie, pretending to sleep, all the while eavesdropping on school administrators. One of those insufferable children who loves both school and church and prefers the company of adults to that of his peers, I took great comfort from the semi-intelligible conversations I overheard while recovering from my playground histrionics.

Medicine seemed to me a kind of sorcery. Whenever my brother or I complained of an earache or sore throat, my father would go to the hall closet and take down the leather satchel from the shelf above the coats. He'd owned it since his days in medical school, and the satchel's brass clasp was deeply tarnished, its leather corners scuffed, the stitching of its handles frayed, signs of age that only made it seem all the more numinous. Inside, disassembled and nested in their cases, were the essential tools of my father's mysterious art—the little illuminated magnifying glass with a snout like an anteater's through which he would inspect our inner ears, the stethoscope, the strange calipers that I never saw him use. I loved the expression

that appeared on his face when he held the drum of his stethoscope to my chest and listened. He'd purse his lips, scrunch his
nose up so that his glasses rose, and cock first one bushy eye-
brow, then the other. "Deep breath," he'd say, then move the
cold metal disk to another spot. "Again." For as long as this ceremony lasted, I felt content, cured. Some of the tests he conducted on us were purely for our amusement. We liked him to
tap us on the knee with his little rubber tomahawk, because
this is what doctors in cartoons always did, and as in cartoons,
we'd kick like chorus girls as soon as the mallet struck.

Saturday mornings when my father was on call, I would
sometimes accompany him on his rounds. He would introduce
me to the nurses, who would crack jokes about the handsome
new surgical intern, meaning me, or ask whether I was going
to be a doctor like my father when I grew up, to which I would
reply, no, I was going to be a veterinarian. When an emergency
arose, or my father had to visit a patient too sick for me to see,
he would leave me in the television lounge. There, sitting cross-
legged on the carpeted floor, I would watch old Shirley Temple
movies or episodes of *The Little Rascals* in the company of cancer patients hairless and emaciated from chemotherapy, I.V.
bags floating abstractly above them. When my father returned,
he would take me to get an apple fritter in the cafeteria, and
then, if there was time and I was good, we'd go see the white
lab rabbits, doomed and ghostly creatures that stared out at me
from inside their metal cages with their tiny pink eyes. I would
poke my finger through the grate and try to pet their noses, all
the while talking to them in what I hoped were soothing tones.

At the hospital, wearing his doctor costume, my father
seemed to transform into a superhero—the soles of his wing-

tips resounding on the polished linoleum as he navigated our way through the labyrinthine halls, his white lab coat sweeping behind him like a cape. His own hero, aside from my grandfather, was the German doctor and pacifist Albert Schweitzer. On a shelf above his desk he kept a small library of books by or about the messianic physician, books with titles like *The Animal World of Albert Schweitzer, The Psychiatric Study of Jesus,* and *On the Edge of the Primeval Forest.* One of these volumes consisted almost entirely of photographs documenting the hospital Schweitzer and his wife had built in the jungles of Africa. Secretly, when I was alone, I liked to take this book down and flip through its crackling pages. In one photograph the laundered bandages of lepers hang from a clothesline. Glowing in the sunlight, they look like the shed skins of giant, luminous snakes. In another, Schweitzer appears to be conversing with two enormous pelicans, as otherworldly as any creatures I had ever seen. Among his patients, Schweitzer resembled some European imperialist's idea of God. Without the captions, one might have guessed that this white fellow in the white suit and white handlebar mustache was not a physician making his rounds but an overseer inspecting his plantation. The pictures that interested me most were the portraits of the diseased and dying—children with distended bellies, women with eye sockets like caves, men with tumorous growths, shiny and puckered like semi-inflated balloons, blossoming from their necks. There's a dark magic in such voyeurism, as if by glimpsing these horrors we might inoculate ourselves against them.

Compared with the tropical illnesses Schweitzer's patients suffered from, my rash of poison oak seemed laughably benign. Nevertheless, it reminded me of pictures I'd seen of smallpox victims, their skin covered in blisters nearly as large as gum-drops. There were aspects of my rash that I enjoyed: the forbidden pleasure of scratching, or the feel of the topography of my own disfigurement, or the oatmeal bath that my mother drew for me one night. A bath of oatmeal! It was like something out of a fairy tale. I sank into its glutinous warmth, which according to my mother would absorb the poisonous oils from my inflamed skin. When she'd decided I'd soaked long enough, I rose out of the porridge like Adam from the dust, gray clumps dripping from my arms, oozing down my legs. After pouring water over my head with a saucepan and toweling me dry, my mother began daubing me all over with a cotton ball dipped in calamine lotion.

This was among the most sensually pleasurable experiences of my life. Children may be morally innocent, but they are not immune to the erogenous. Wasn't my tumble through the grass erotic? Isn't sex bewildering? To this day, I can remember the odor of calamine, the sticky sound of the cotton unpeeling from my skin, the cold wet kiss of it on my arms and legs, on my swollen eyelids, on my rashy scrotum. Once she'd finished, my mother instructed me to stand in the hot air gusting from the heating vent while I waited for the lotion to form a crust, which it shortly did, baking into a new pink skin that cracked and flaked when I moved, as if I were sloughing it.

Sickness, health—these were the two great leitmotifs of my childhood, the poles that had electrified our family's private life. The winter my parents decided to marry, my father, in California on a leave of absence from the University of Illinois medical school, had begun experiencing dizzy spells so acute he was unable to stand. His doctors admitted him in order to test for brain cancer, the prospect of which proved to be the decisive factor in my mother's assent to his proposal, or so she now says. His dizziness turned out to be a symptom of labyrinthitis, a viral infection of the inner ear, but there, in the hospital, in crisis, when he'd asked her to marry him, she had imagined he was terminally ill. He had needed her. How could she abandon him now? So she gave up her mutually exclusive dreams—of chasing Dongho Kim, going to medical school, or becoming a nun—and sacrificed herself to my father instead. Even before the vows were consecrated, the gradual alienation that would eventuate in divorce had begun. My father's recovery denied my mother's life the meaning and purpose his dying had given it, and she never found a suitable replacement—except when my brother or I fell ill.

Messiah

Families, like empires, decline slowly from within, though an outside event—the domestic equivalent of a barbarian invasion, an erupting volcano, or the crucifixion of a charismatic—can sometimes precipitate the collapse. Every Christmas, the church choir in which my father sang bass drove three hours northeast to Covelo, California, a small ranching town nestled in the mountains of the coastal range. Locals would provide lodging to choristers and their families, and in exchange the choir would give a free performance of Handel's *Messiah* in the town meeting hall. For my father, these trips were nostalgic pilgrimages, antidotes to homesickness, Covelo an approximation of the small farm towns he remembered from his Midwestern boyhood, the performances of the "Hallelujah" Chorus substitutes for his youthful dream of playing trombone in a symphony orchestra, a dream he'd set aside, pragmatically, for medicine.

In December of 1979, when I was seven years old, our family was billeted in the home of a rancher whose name I have since forgotten. On the morning of the concert, my father, my brother, and I helped our host and his two sons feed the cattle. We loaded bales of hay onto an old flatbed truck and drove out to the pastures, my father behind the wheel, the rest of us in back. When the rancher snapped off the baling wire with his shears, the bricks of hay came apart in slices, and we'd hurl these into the feeding troughs that ran like gutters along either side of the road.

The truck ambled along so slowly you could have kept up with it on foot. Emboldened, perhaps, by this slow pace, my brother climbed down onto the running board at the base of the passenger door, hung from the mirror like a conductor from a train, and waved for my benefit. His hair was long and curly then, like the hair of angels in paintings, and the breeze feathered it against his cheeks; the lenses of his glasses shone. This stunt of his looked to me like great fun, and when he had clambered back up and resumed tossing hay, I decided that it was my turn. Getting down wasn't hard, and riding on the running board was as easy as riding a cable car down California Street. From across the fields, cattle were converging upon the fence, lowing to one another, extending their enormous heads through the slats, plunging their muzzles into the troughs. Earlier that morning, I'd been allowed to give a newborn calf a bottle of milk. It had suckled noisily, desperately, tugging the bottle almost from my hand, its eyes wild with appetite. There was a white whorl of fur at the center of its forehead that was satisfying to pet. I'd wanted to stay at the barn, feeding the calf, but my father, eager to pass on the knowledge of farm work he'd inherited from his forebears, had convinced me to come along for the ride, so here I was, standing on the running board of an old truck on a bright, cold December morning pungent with manure, the fields stretching away in all directions toward the snow-capped mountains in the distance. I hollered "hello" to my father through the glass of the passenger window, but he kept his eyes on the road. The truck was rattling so loudly he couldn't hear me. Climbing back up to the truck's bed proved to be the hard part. There was a wooden panel behind the cab like a headboard. You had to grab hold of it and hoist yourself, and the corner of it was worn smooth. I hung from it for a moment by my fingertips, trying to get a purchase with my feet. Then the truck bounced, and I fell beneath its wheels.

I remember my back hitting the road. Then people were leaping from the bed of the truck and running up the road toward me. My father kept driving, unaware. Then he was beside me, pulling my pants down, checking for bleeding. There were tire treads imprinted on my legs. I chanted the words "help me" over and over. My father lifted me into his arms. For a moment I thought that he was going to set me on my feet to see if I could stand, and I screamed. Then we were in the cab of a truck, the rancher at the wheel, my father in the passenger seat, holding me. The only doctor in the area happened to be out of town, but someone managed to find a spare key to his clinic, and my father took me there. Lying on a table, I watched him cut my shirt off with scissors, my favorite shirt, striped in alternating bands of color. My father wrapped my legs in plaster splints. People were helping him. They made a bed for me in the back of our station wagon. I remember the patterned lining of the sleeping bag they spread over me, red with bounding stags. While my father drove as fast, he has since told me, as he has ever driven, I stared up out the rear window at the sky and the telephone wires, which seemed to be racing alongside us, leaping and dipping like dolphins. At one point, my mother helped me urinate into a jar. Then there were streetlights overhead, steep hills, buildings, a hospital, a world of fluorescent brightness through which I traveled on a gurney to strange rooms where strange hands lifted me onto cold tables, draped me in a lead apron, wrapped me like a mummy in strips of wet plaster all the way to my collarbone, so that, immobilized, I wouldn't damage the nerves running up my legs and spine.

Despite the body cast, my injuries were relatively minor. I'd fractured the femur in my left leg, torn ligaments in my right one. The double-wide rear tires of the truck had distributed the weight. If they'd passed an inch lower, my knees would have been crushed; a few inches higher and the wheels would have shattered my pelvis. My classmates composed letters to me, written in crayon on paper with inch-high lines, and illustrated them with pictures of a stick figure squashed beneath the wheels of a two-dimensional truck. A delegation was sent to deliver these letters to me, along with a teddy bear. Within a few weeks, I returned to school in a wheelchair, its back canted and its footrest raised to accommodate the supine posture of my cast. My teachers made other kids sharpen my pencil, or fetch my lunch bag from my locker, and when I needed to use the toilet, my brother would be summoned from the fourth-grade homeroom to help. The shape and texture of the plaster tended to make pants slide down, so my mother dressed me in an extra-large pair of bib overalls. My brother would unbuckle the shoulder straps, then hold me up while I peed. The plaster edges of the hole my doctor had left in the cast for this purpose were sharp, and I cut myself on it once or twice, but aside from this wound, infirmity suited me fine. I would have preferred it to take longer for my legs to recover. The accident made me special, beloved, almost holy.

Lapsus

Lucifer falls, Alice falls, so does Icarus. Humpty Dumpty falls. The giant in "Jack and the Beanstalk" falls. Jack and Jill fall. The Titans tumble earthward for nine days straight. Elpenor slips headlong from Circe's roof. Adam and Eve supposedly fall, though in fact the theological idea of a lapse into sin is Christian in origin, the necessary precondition for rapture. We must fall so that Christ can raise us. Read Genesis, however, and you'll see that the authors of the Hebrew scriptures, their imaginations defined perhaps by the long horizons of the Fertile Crescent, conceive of expulsion in lateral terms. The central metaphor is not descent but exile. Still, the experience of falling is so fundamental that it lends itself to moral and existential embellishment.

Witnessed or not, an accidental fall entails a loss of dignity. Our upright posture most distinguishes *Homo erectus* from that class of creatures that the Bible identifies as "creeping," and no animal is creepier than that enigmatic serpent whose curse it is to crawl upon the ground, just as no animal topples more easily than we do. Quadrupeds wobble and trip when newborn, but rarely thereafter. Just think what a horrific sight it is to see a racehorse go down. Implicit in the biblical stories is a kind of hierarchy of being that seems to mirror the human body cosmologically. I suspect that Zeus and Baal and Yahweh Himself may be associated with mountaintops and clouds in part because our eyes are among our own most altitudinous organs. To be human is to defy gravity. To be a snake is to embrace it. The snake is thus our anatomical opposite, though when we fall—or sleep, or have sex, or die—we assume a serpentine posture, a fact implicit in the symbolism of Genesis.

Only with the Hellenic distinction between the body and the spirit could we imagine the dead ascending like helium balloons into the sky. The flight of Icarus is not merely an allegory about human ambition. It is an allegory about our ambition to slip our mortal bonds. Only the soul may ascend; the body must plummet. To be earthbound is to be deathbound. In the theater of battle to *fall* means to *die*. The same logic governs the collapse of architecture and empires, those collective attempts to defy gravity and time. But there is also a pleasure in falling, in giving in, in assenting to gravity's pull. Although we can fall into disgrace, or obscurity, we can also fall into a trance, or sleep, or love. What these experiences have in common is the surrendering of will—to music, or to unconsciousness, or to another. These are all varieties of bewilderment. In the absence of pain, falling ill can accord some of the same pleasures as falling in love. There is a voluptuousness to illness, the eros of the infantile. Even seemingly disastrous falls can be accompanied by the joy of relief or the exhilaration of chaos.

Once, when I was fourteen years old, the year I left my native city for good, some friends and I stole a grocery cart, wheeled it to a precipice overlooking San Francisco Bay, and launched it into the sky. We did this for the hell of it, for the thrill of watching something big and heavy fall. As the cart plummeted, we glimpsed far more vividly than otherwise what it would be like for our own bodies to plunge. The cart's descent lasted surprisingly long. Every few moments it ricocheted off the face of the cliff and spun wildly, dust exploding into the air. When it finally reached sea level, the splash was barely noticeable, an anticlimactic puff of spray, nothing more. For a few seconds, it remained visible in the shallows, as if threatening to float. Then a wave came in and made it disappear.

S.O.S.

My mother blamed my father for my accident. He'd been driving after all and had nearly killed me, a thought that haunts him to this day. Despite her rancor, for the few months of my convalescence, her life was purposeful; thereafter, it fell apart. Her depression returned. Within a year she'd moved into an apartment of her own, this time for good. "If you are ready to leave father and mother, and brother and sister, and wife and child and friends, and never see them again," says Thoreau, paraphrasing Jesus, "then you are ready for a walk." God still stalks the American Eden, forest Christians seem to believe, and if we keep walking, we may yet find Him there. Or maybe that isn't quite it. Maybe it's an absentee divinity that forest Christians prefer, a creator who does not forbid or punish or command, who does not go walking in his garden in search of those who've sinned. Compared with fathers and mothers, and brothers and sisters, and wives—not to mention husbands and sons—trees make few demands, and you can hear whatever your heart desires in the lyrical soughing of their branches.

In fifth grade, two years after the divorce, I resolved to become a priest. I wrote a research paper about near-death experiences. Like Michael Landon, who played an angel on television, I grew my hair long. I tried reading the Bible from the beginning but only made it as far as Genesis 22, the sacrifice of Isaac. I built an altar in our backyard out of mud and bricks. I knelt before it and prayed. The leaves of the plum tree shook, the telephone wires swayed in the fog, a phone rang in a neighbor's house, but the skies did not open, the earth did not quake, flames did not dance upon my altar, an angel of the Lord did not call my name.

I started my own nongovernmental organization, a school club called S.O.S. for Save Our Seas, that managed to raise $70 in singles and change, which I personally delivered in a brown paper bag to the offices of Greenpeace. I hung posters of harp seals and humpback whales on my bedroom walls. I preached about the sins of CFCs and six-pack rings, the virtues of recycling. I delivered apocalyptic oral reports about the massacre of dolphins, describing in detail how Japanese fishermen would harpoon one of these beautiful, intelligent creatures and hang it from the mast of their ship by its tail so that it would call out, summoning others to its rescue, and to slaughter.

For forest Christians such abominations are inescapably symbolic. This was not merely an illegal dolphin hunt I was preaching about. This was the Slaughter of the Innocent, environmentalism as passion play. Think of the iconography: the bludgeoned seal pup trailing blood across the snow, the elephant defaced by poachers, the corpses of dolphins arranged at the pearly fringes of a blood-red tide in as orderly a fashion as graves in a cemetery—or headless pigeons atop an altar. And I did not simply pity the slaughtered innocent; truth was, I envied them, much as I did Christ, forsaken but nonetheless beloved on his cross. Didn't his mother weep for him even as he wept for us?

How I longed for rapture! To be seized, carried off. To fall prey, ecstatically, to God. Maybe my mother did too. Maybe that was the treasure she went hunting for, the object of her long desire. Alas, even after the divorce, rapture continued to elude her. An empty garden was not enough. Neither music nor voices could be heard in the swaying eucalyptus branches, only wind, only noise. *"Contact! Contact!"* Thoreau shouted at the heavens after summiting Mount Katahdin. *"Who* are we? *where* are we?"* And the heavens did not reply.

In 1981, a year after moving into a room of her own, my mother opened a bottle of tricyclic antidepressants. She took one. And then another. Until the entire bottle was gone. And then she lay down and went to sleep. Yes, the mass of men lead lives of quiet desperation; the mass of women too. But what if when you go out walking into the forenoon, the quiet desperation follows you? What if, like my mother, you quit one job after another, take one long walk after another, spend your whole life sauntering toward the Holy Land never to arrive?

Acrobatics

I sometimes wish I could go back in time and dissuade my parents from marrying. "Go ahead and join the convent!" I would tell my mother, "Don't marry Dad. Forget Dongho Kim too. Marry that skinny guy up there on the cross! He'll never die on you, and he won't suddenly get better, either. He'll never climb down, heal his own wounds, want to have sex, snore loudly beside you, shower, shave, get dressed for work. He'll always be right up there dying." I'd tell my father not to mistake my mother for his angel of mercy; otherwise he would end up becoming hers.

And if this failed to frighten him, if he insisted that he had fallen in love with this beautiful girl (for my mother was beautiful, dark-haired and small like Audrey Hepburn), I would tell him how, one day not long after their divorce, for reasons he would come to regard as miraculous, he would drive by her apartment building and notice that she'd forgotten to move her car, which was parked illegally in a street-cleaning zone. He would stop then, not out of love but out of foreboding, and ring her doorbell. When no one answered, he'd find a pay phone and call her psychiatrist, who'd share his foreboding. How the superintendent would let my father into his ex-wife's small apartment, and, sure enough, there, in those quiet, almost empty rooms, he would find her unconscious and almost dead.

He would struggle to find a pulse. When he did, it would be the faintest fluttering at her wrist. I would tell him about the night, a few months later, after her release from the psychiatric ward, when, seemingly by accident, she'd be hit by a van while crossing the street in the fog. Her head would strike the pavement first. She would forget everything for a while, even his face, even speech, even me. She would never fully recover from this fall.

If this still had not sufficiently impressed him, I would tell him how she would let her nursing license expire; how she would move from menial job to menial job, invariably quitting or getting herself fired when her employers refused to enact whatever unlikely reforms my mother required of them. She would wander from one rented room to another, all the while sending her sons letters describing the various shortcomings of her employers, the pretty things she'd noticed on her nature walks, and the manifold physical ailments, real and imaginary, that afflicted her. I'd tell my father how, in January of 1995, fifteen years after the divorce, unemployed and too broke to afford a room at the Thrift O Tel, that beautiful young student nurse he'd fallen in love with would get into her ancient Toyota and drive across the eastern United States in a snowstorm to Boston, where, alone, in a small and almost empty apartment in Allston, her younger son was working on both a master's degree and a drinking habit. She would show up on his doorstep seeking sanctuary, and, ruefully, he would let her in. I imagine telling my youthful, lovelorn father all of this, but who am I fooling? The past creates us and we are powerless to change it. We can only—if we are very persistent and very lucky and usually not even then—change ourselves.

There is a riddle I remember from my childhood. It went like this: "The music stopped, and she died." Provided with these two facts, you were supposed to deduce the connection between them. Who was she? Why did the music stop? What music? The catch was, you could ask only yes or no questions. That was the rule. Were the interruption in the music and her death merely coincidental? No. Did the stopping of the music somehow cause her death? Yes. Through such interrogation, you would eventually grope your way toward the answer, or else you would grow impatient and persuade the person telling the riddle to divulge it: She was a blindfolded tightrope walker. The musicians provided her cues. When they stopped playing, it was supposed to indicate that she'd safely reached the end of the rope and could step onto the platform. But the musicians had stopped playing too soon, and the tightrope walker had stepped into thin air. Hence, "The music stopped, and she died." I never liked this riddle. The answer seemed elaborate but arbitrary. It raised as many questions as it answered. Why did the musicians stop playing? Why did the tightrope walker need a cue? Wouldn't she have been able to feel the end of the rope with her foot? Why was there no net? Because this was a riddle, because evidence could not be gathered and assessed, there were no answers to questions such as these. There were only speculations.

AND YET

Driving home from Detroit the other day, through the familiar scenery along I-94, past the colossal replica of a Uniroyal tire—that great black O beside Mile 205—I found myself unable to form a single thought that did not trail after it the words "and yet." Those words are a synapse between two thoughts. The second thought qualifies and complicates the first. And yet I can't help hearing time ticking in the phrase. "Yet" also means "still." As in, *For all that has happened during the last four centuries, for all the changes that have taken place on its banks, the Detroit River yet flows, discharging into Lake Erie 1,373,694 gallons of water every second.*

The Uniroyal tire beside I-94 is the size of a Ferris wheel—precisely the size of a Ferris wheel, because it used to be one. It came into the world as a Ferris wheel made to look like a colossal tire. The Uniroyal tire company built it for the 1964 World's Fair in Queens, New York. After the fair ended, the company repurposed the carnival ride as a monument and advertisement, erecting it beside I-94 where it still resides, encircled by a fence topped with razor wire. In 1998, an advertising team had a construction crew affix to it an ersatz nail the size of a lamppost. The nail was part of a promotional campaign for a new line of tires supposedly resistant to puncture. It has since been removed—why, I'm not sure, but I know that if I'd caught a glimpse of a colossal nail poking from a colossal tire, I would not have thought, *I need to buy new tires.*

As I passed the airport, the grand implausibility of a jumbo jet was lowering its wheels overhead. It was so low, so giant, so close—you could see the rivets on the wing flaps—that I couldn't help imagining a disaster, the jet crash-landing on the interstate, wheels touching down among the speeding cars. And yet the leafless trees under the power lines continued to strain their black branches into the atmosphere. A billboard continued to advertise the Motor City Casino (tagline: *Cheat on your life*). A different billboard continued to offer commuters a view of a sunset over a Great Lake and the words PURE MICH-IGAN. And the jumbo jet continued its descent, uneventfully.

These days I often find myself wondering at the world. I'll be driving down I-94, looking out at the billboards and the leaf-less trees, thinking to myself: *How did it come to be this way? Precisely this way? And how did I end up precisely here of all places, speeding down I-94 in an aging station wagon with a dented fender, a manic-depressive heater (dormant or else on at full blast), and a busted windshield wiper, the rubber blade a black noodle lashing ineffectually across the salty smear of snowmelt aerosolized by the tires of passing semis?*

For the last several years, I've been teaching at Detroit's pub-lic university, a venerable institution that dates to Reconstruc-tion. It began as the Detroit Medical College, founded in 1868, a date I know well because it appears—beneath the university's logo, a stylized green *W* that resembles the winged silhouette of a bat—on the interfaces of the classroom computers. Like the county that encompasses Detroit, the university is named

for Anthony Wayne, general in the Revolutionary War, nick-
named "Mad Anthony" by a resentful malingerer he'd court-
martialed. So far as eighteenth-century *noms de guerre* go,
"Mad Anthony" is hard to beat. Near the end of his career,
Wayne led a campaign against the Algonquian-speaking
nations of the Great Lakes, violently pacifying a native alliance
led by a previously triumphant Miami warrior named Little
Turtle, conquering much of the territory from which the states
of Ohio, Indiana, and Michigan would soon be carved. And
yet, at age fifty-one, just two years after his victory in the Battle
of Fallen Timbers, which took place near present-day Toledo,
Mad Anthony died in a cabin on the Lake Erie coast—of gout,
a disease associated with a diet rich in red meat and liquor. Federal officials memorialized him by sprinkling his name all over
the newly expanded map. His body they buried in a wooden
coffin across which they'd spelled out his initials in brass tacks.
Twelve years later, Wayne's children arranged to have his disin-
terred remains shipped home across Pennsylvania. The doctor
in charge of the exhumation, finding the corpse to be surprisingly well preserved, boiled the rotting flesh from the old general's bones. From this history I've learned a lesson resembling
an aphorism: A skeleton is easier to transport through rough
terrain than a corpse.

Not long ago, I spent some time learning about underwater
archaeology. On land, Michigan's acidic soil and the American habit of renovation have together erased much of the past.
After traveling with underwater archaeologists, I kept wishing that I could tie a side-scan sonar to the rear bumper of my
station wagon when I drove around the Midwest. A side-scan
sonar is a device that underwater archaeologists tow behind

their research vessels while searching the seabed for sunken relics. In the parlance of underwater archaeologists, surveying the seabed is "mowing the lawn." You set a bearing and motor toward the horizon for a while. Then you pull a 180 and motor back. Pull another 180, and so on. All the while, the side-scan sonar, which in form resembles a miniature torpedo, is porpoising along beneath the turbid surface of the wake, beaming the depths with pulses of sound. From the data it collects, underwater archaeologists assemble maps out of graphic strips of roughly equal width, converting yards of seabed or lakebed to millimeters of ink, each strip representing a single pass. In these graphic strips, these pixelated ribbons, the bottom of a lake or sea resembles the surface of some distant planet as viewed by an orbiting satellite. Assembled, the strips show variations in color that call to mind the striped pattern of a freshly mown lawn, those bands of grass, alternatingly dark green and light. Underwater archaeologists call the side-scan sonar the towfish, which is confusing, since it is what they fish with when they go fishing for relics—the tracking device, not the prey.

Shortly after I began teaching at the city university, I learned about one of my predecessors on the faculty, an experimental geographer named William Bunge. Known to colleagues by the nickname "Wild Bill," in his first book, *Theoretical Geography*, now considered a classic of spatial science, Bunge attempted to discover "morphological laws" that would fill "our consciousness" with the "symmetry and ordered beauty" of "our planet, Earth." And yet, after moving to Detroit from Iowa in 1963 and witnessing the unrest that roiled cities of the industrial Midwest in the wake of the civil rights movement, Bunge experienced an apostasy. Abandoning planetary revelations for "micro-historical-regional" ones and supplementing spatial science with field work, he proposed to create a "humanistic," as opposed to a physical, geography. He sought to make visible previously invisible features in the urban landscape.

Bunge's most famous maps are those made under the auspices of the Detroit Geographical Expedition and Institute, which he helped found. The institute trained Detroiters to work as documentarians and cartographers of their own neighborhoods. "The purpose of the Expedition is to help the human species most directly," Bunge wrote. "It is a geography that tends to shock because it includes the full range of human experience on the earth's surface; not just the recreation land, but the blighted land; not just the affluent, but the poor; not just the beautiful, but the ugly." From the expedition's field work, Bunge made maps that he collected and commented upon in a pair of volumes, *An Atlas of Love and Hate: Detroit Geographies* and *Fitzgerald: Geography of a Revolution,* that have since influenced the field of infographics as well as geography. One map shows "where commuters run over black children." Another charts the "region of rat-bitten babies." A third illustrates the "direction of money transfers in Metropolitan Detroit"—from inner city to outer suburbs. In 1969 the university fired Bunge for reasons controversial and opaque. The official grounds for dismissal: a habit of cursing in class. Unofficially, some colleagues blamed his history of unprofessional belligerence; supporters blamed his politics. Blacklisted in 1970 by the House Committee on Internal Security (formerly the House Un-American Activities Committee), he fled to Canada, where he became an itinerant scholar, landing and losing teaching appointments before renouncing academia altogether. By the late 1970s, he was a cabdriver in Quebec. Cabdrivers, he came to believe, were true geographers. On a typewriter he kept in his taxi, he continued to write, and in 1988 he published his last book, *Nuclear War Atlas*, a late Cold War–era pacifist's manifesto in the form of maps and charts. The book's "underlying philosophy is some nuclear-aged version of my childhood philosopher, the Jew, Jesus Christ, who also preached against killing children," he wrote to the *Journal of Geography* in response to a hostile review. The last mention of him I could find in newspaper archives dates from the late 1990s, when he ran for the Canadian parliament on the Communist Party ticket and lost. Aside from a few appearances at geographical conferences, he'd since become a recluse, rumored to be living in the vicinity of Arthabaska, Quebec, a small town an hour's drive northeast of Montreal, not far from the south bank of the Saint Lawrence River. I'd been meaning to go there and look for him, but by the time I got around to it, an Internet search returned an obituary.

In one of the courses I teach at the university, I always assign Virginia Woolf's essay "Street Haunting," in which Woolf narrates and meditates upon a walk she took through London one winter night almost a century ago. Into her wintry observations, memories of warmer months intrude. "Is the true self this which stands on the pavement in January, or that which bends over the balcony in June?" she wonders. "Am I here, or am I there? Or is the true self neither this nor that, neither here nor there, but something so varied and wandering that it is only when we give the rein to its wishes and let it take its way unimpeded that we are indeed ourselves?"

Detroit these days bears little obvious resemblance to London. The sediment of recorded history has had less time to accumulate along these riverbanks, and much of the wealth that once made buildings spring from this soil has washed away. And yet a winter walk through Detroit still has much in common with a winter walk through London. Sidewalks are sidewalks, snow is snow, steps are steps. It is my supposition that our experience of time is determined by the speed at which we move, and that the human mind therefore evolved to move through the world at approximately three miles per hour.

I ask my students to follow Woolf's example by taking walks and, while walking, to take notes. From those notes they are to re-create their walks for readers, the sights and the sounds, but also their own reactions to the sights and sounds, their unbidden memories and thoughts. If they wish, they may take a ride on a bus or a train instead. Car travel I forbid. Whatever the lessons in geography cabdrivers learn, for most of us, car travel tends to isolate the mind and blur the senses, and it is a bad idea to take notes while driving. And yet most weeks the hours I spend commuting are the only hours in which I let my own mind wander, I walk less than I used to, and in the last several years, I've driven all over the interior of the continent, following the lake shores and riverbanks.

In the dispatches my students write about their walks, I've caught glimpses of neighborhoods and homes I'll never visit. Greater Detroit is a balkanized place. My students come from all over the metropolitan area, and from beyond it. They take their walks at different hours as well as in different neighborhoods, some by day, some after sundown, and yet in my mind, as I read them one after the other, their essays become simultaneous. Instead of making Detroit and the region more real to me, the glimpses I catch in their essays have made me feel as if I were haunting the place where I live and work, a ghost viewing the city and region from on high through a toy kaleidoscope equipped with a zoom lens. Give the cylinder a turn and the fragmentary images tumble. Patterns emerge. Images of snowy, salted sidewalks and bare tree branches recur, as do puddles of slush, trash snagged in the empty diamonds of hurricane fences. My students often write sentences that are lovely, and even some of their unlovely sentences are moving to me. All human lives are poignant when seen intimately but from a distance. This may help explain the widespread belief, contradicted by so much evidence, in a loving God.

Acknowledgments

For this book, I owe my biggest debt of gratitude to Matt Weiland, who shared and shaped a vision and gave these essays an excellent home. Thanks, as well, to the rest of the team at W. W. Norton: Zarina Patwa, Fred Weimer, Susan Sanfrey, Erin Reilly, Lauren Abbate, Sarahmay Wilkinson, Steve Colca, Rose Sheehan, and Jason Storms. I remain grateful to Josh Kendall, who edited *Moby-Duck* (and now edits fiction for Mulholland Books), and to all the folks at Viking. From the start, I've been lucky to have Heather Schroder of Compass Talent in my corner as agent and friend.

Tom Bissell was the first reader of the first complete draft of "Falling," whose subjects I'd struggled to write about for many years. I might have given up were it not for Tom's encouragement. At *Harper's*, the editors of essays included here were, in the following order, John Jeremiah Sullivan, Roger Hodge, Jeremy Keehn, and Christopher Cox. I am especially grateful to Roger, who also edited two essays that grew into my first book. I'm indebted to many other *Harper's* veterans, contributors as well as editors. Mark Slouka, Rebecca Solnit, Wyatt Mason, and Jeff Sharlet offered wisdom and friendship when I sorely needed it. Ted Ross fact-checked "Falling" and later, as an editor at the *New Republic*, asked me to write about Thoreau.

Jennifer Szalai, after moving to the *New York Times Book Review*, assigned me to write about essay collections by Annie Dillard and Marilynne Robinson.

Parul Sehgal of the *New York Times* somehow knew that woolly mammoths would be for me an irresistible subject. At *Lapham's Quarterly*, I need to thank above all Lewis Lapham, for creating that singular journal and for running an excerpt of "A Romance of Rust" under the title "Lost Symbols." Kira Brunner Don also lent support, and Henry Freedland piloted me skillfully through the history of water-writing. Paul Reyes has been working editorial wonders since taking the helm of the *Virginia Quarterly Review*, and I'm grateful that he shared some portion of my fascination with the Saint Lawrence River and the obscure sport of ice canoeing. Thank you to Dinty W. Moore and the rest of the team at *Brevity*. My editor at the *New York Times Magazine* is Claire Gutierrez. She, Jessica Lustig, and Bill Wasik helped me navigate the controversies that followed the poisoning of Flint's water, as did the fact-checking team led by Nanditha Rodrigo.

At Boston University, I briefly worked as an assistant to Elie Wiesel, who told me that his favorite two words in English were "and yet." At the University of Michigan, where this book began, I met a number of guides and a great many kindred spirits. Three of these essays emerged from drafts I wrote while studying creative nonfiction with Eileen Pollack and poetry with Linda Gregerson, Richard Tillinghast, and Lorna Goodison. Nicholas Delbanco gave me generous notes. Discussions in a seminar taught by Charles Baxter were an influence, as were discussions with John Knott about the literature of the American wilderness, as were conversations with poets

Rachel Richardson and Suzanne Hancock. I owe an even older debt to T. S. McMillin, author of *The Meaning of Rivers: Flow and Reflection in American Literature*. Since my return to Michigan, Jeremiah Chamberlin and I have had many conversations about nonfiction, some of them conducted in public at a special nonfiction session of the Sozopol Seminars on the shores of the Black Sea. David Morse gave me notes on several first drafts. Claudia Kraus Piper shared wisdom.

When I began publishing these essays, I was on the faculty of Friends Seminary, where I had the good fortune to learn and practice the art of teaching in the company of virtuosos like Phil Schwartz, Sarah Spieldenner, Camille Guthrie, Ben Frisch, and Maria Fahey. It was during my first semester at Friends that a precociously erudite student named Hannah Frank elected to take the first nonfiction class I attempted to teach. I still remember one discussion we had that semester, concerning the hazards of nostalgia in artistic remembrances of childhood— hazards that, at seventeen, she'd already given much thought. By the time she died in 2017, at thirty-three, with no forewarning, of bacterial meningitis, Hannah had become a film scholar and a professor, a specialist in the material history of twentieth-century animation who had just begun to share her own mature work with the world. In 2019, the University of California Press posthumously published Hannah's first book, *Frame by Frame: A Materialist Aesthetics of Animated Cartoons*. When my copy arrived in the mail, I felt as if I'd received a letter from a ghost. There was her voice on the page, as lively as ever.

I finished this book while on the writing faculty of Wayne State University, where I've also had the good fortune to work alongside virtuosos—Caroline Maun, Natalie Bakopoulos, Jamaal May, Jeff Pruchnic (who introduced me to the work of William Bunge), et al.—and with students who are the reason I love my job. They have affirmed my faith in that beleaguered institution, the public university.

Dan Fenster, after Didionizing Detroit for his M.A. thesis, provided research assistance as well as a ride across the Mississippi Delta in his amazing van, may it rest in peace. Ongoing conversations and correspondence with LaToya Faulk and Ariel Mokdad have helped me a great deal to think about the teaching of nonfiction. Benjamin Turner, desperado poet and philosopher, provided teaching assistance, as did pigeon-fancying archaeologist-of-the-ordinary and reading-series impresario Connor Newton. With Laura Kraftowitz and Robert Laidler, I share the wish that all cities might become cities of asylum, Detroit included.

I've traveled with several people whose names do not appear in the preceding pages: David Porter took me sailing on Lake Erie. Archaeologist John O'Shea let me ride along during an underwater excavation of the Alpena-Amberley Ridge. An archaeological team at Thunder Bay National Marine Sanctuary also let me accompany them aboard a research vessel. Christopher Jerde of Notre Dame took me carp hunting on the Des Plaines River, outflow of the Chicago Sanitary and Ship Canal. At one point, I thought I might write about the dwindling wolves of Isle Royale, where I spent a few days learning from John and Leah Vucetich about their longitudinal study of predator-prey population dynamics. With river guide Mike "Big Muddy" Clark I transited the port of St. Louis. On a mapping expedition led by John "Driftwood" Ruskey of the Lower Mississippi Foundation and Mark "River" Peoples of 1 Mississippi, I traveled the last 250 miles of the Lower Mississippi by canoe, camping on mud flats across from the French Quarter and picnicking in the shadow of petrochemical refineries. When Hurricane Patricia interrupted that trip, Marylee Orr of the Louisiana Environmental Action Network provided shelter and sustenance.

Over the years, I received support that made the work possible: a Whiting Award, a National Endowment for the Arts Creative Writing Fellowship, a Knight-Wallace Fellowship from the University of Michigan, and from Wayne State University, a Research Enhancement Program for the Humanities Grant and a Career Development Chair.

It is not always easy to have a writer in the family. I apologize to my parents and siblings for excavating so many memories from the sediment of Mount Davidson, including painful ones. I tried to corroborate them when possible, and to alchemize as well as excavate. John and Pat O'Connor greeted my attempts to make sense of my family with welcome empathy and understanding, answering many questions. Chris and Pam Hohn provided pro bono research assistance and hosted me on repeated visits to Illinois. I owe a special thanks to Tom and Martha Friedlander, whose wild wetlands and museum of rusty implements I still frequent and who continue to instruct me in my amateur botanizing of Midwestern flora.

I am most grateful of all to the three paddlers who've accompanied me in the dented canoe, through rapids and calms: Beth, Bruno, Malachy.

Credits

"Snail Picking" originally appeared in *Brevity*, issue 27, May 2008.

"A Romance of Rust" originally appeared in *Harper's Magazine*, January 2005.

"Revival of the Ice Canoe" originally appeared in *Virginia Quarterly Review*, Winter 2018.

"Watermarks" originally appeared in *Lapham's Quarterly*, Summer 2018.

"Midwest Passage" originally appeared under the title "Reverse Engineering" in *The New York Times Magazine*, February 8, 2015.

"The Zealot" originally appeared in *The New York Times Magazine*, August 21, 2016.

"Mammoth Fever" originally appeared under the title "When They Roamed the Earth" in *The New York Times Book Review*, December 31, 2017.

"Evan S. Connell" originally appeared under the title "Remembering Evan S. Connell (1924–2013)" on the website of *Harper's Magazine*, January 14, 2013.

"Marilynne Robinson" originally appeared under the title "Fierce Convictions" in *The New York Times Book Review*, March 11, 2018.

"Matthew Power" originally appeared under the title "Matt Power: Headlamp a Must" on the website of *Harper's Magazine*, March 19, 2014.

"Henry David Thoreau" originally appeared under the title "Everybody Hates Henry" on the website of *The New Republic*, October 21, 2015.

"Falling" originally appeared in *Harper's Magazine*, April 2008.